SYSTEMATIC DESENSITISATION FOR PANIC AND PHOBIA

SYSTEMATIC DESENSITISATION FOR PANIC AND PHOBIA

An Introduction for Health Professionals

Rhona M. Fear

KARNAC

First published in 2018 by
Karnac Books Ltd
118 Finchley Road, London NW3 5HT

British Library Cataloguing in Publication Data

A C.I.P. for this book is available from the British Library

ISBN 978 1 78220 579 1

Edited, designed and produced by The Studio Publishing Services Ltd
www.publishingservicesuk.co.uk
email: studio@publishingservicesuk.co.uk

www.karnacbooks.com

CONTENTS

ABOUT THE AUTHOR

Rhona Fear BA (Hons), MA, has trained as a psychoanalytic psychotherapist. She still maintains a small psychotherapy practice, although she now concentrates upon writing rather than spending the majority of her time as a practitioner. She specialised for twenty-five years in helping clients in long-term therapy to experience how it feels to have an experience of a "secure base" (Bowlby, 1988) within the therapeutic relationship; many of her clients had suffered from developmental deficiency in terms of attachment experience.

However, her training earlier in her career was eclectic. She initially trained as a counsellor with Relate in 1989, and shortly after this time she completed a masters' degree in counselling studies at the University of Keele. While a student, she became fascinated by the integration debate, and published a number of papers and edited chapters on integration in the nineties. In recent years she has described her theoretical orientation as integrative, and Karnac has published a book outlining her own personal integrative stance: *Attachment Theory: Working Towards Learned Security* (2016).The book begins with a resume of attachment theory, both as promulgated by Bowlby and then developed since his death by others. It moves on to cover some of the causes of developmental deficit. Fear next puts forward an integration of Bowlby's attachment theory along with Stolorow, Brandchaft, and Atwood's intersubjective perspective and Kohut's psychology of the self. The book ends with a number of case studies of individuals with whom she has worked in long-term therapy; they exemplify the integrative stance that she has employed in her practice in recent years.

She has always maintained a strong interest in working with clients suffering from panic disorder and phobias—perhaps partially because she suffered severely from agoraphobia herself in her twenties, and was delighted to recover fully with the help of a dedicated psychologist who taught her the systematic desensitisation programme that she advocates in this book. Despite her leanings towards an analytic modality, she believes that in cases of panic and phobia a cognitive behavioural approach serves the client well.

She achieved a first class honours degree in political science, and over the years has put this into use by taking an active part in both representative democracy and pressure group politics. From a political standpoint, she believes that this book is particularly appropriate because of the lack of resources in the NHS in the recent climate of cutbacks within the British Government. She hopes by making this resource available that more sufferers of panic and phobia will be able to access a method by which they can recover from such disabling illnesses.

Karnac published her first book, *The Oedipus Complex: Solutions or Resolutions?* in 2015. This promulgates the notion that there is a causal correlation between the individual's attachment schema and the temporary, defensive "solution" he attempts to make in order to come to terms with his unresolved Oedipus complex. The book is in two parts: the first part covers an exposition of Freudian, Kleinian, and feminist theory, while in the second part Fear presents six case studies. These case studies aim to exemplify how some individuals achieve a permanent "resolution" of the complex through their work in therapy, thus enabling them to abandon their temporary defensive "solution" as its structure breaks down.

INTRODUCTION

I hope that it will prove beneficial in writing this book that during my early adult years I suffered severely from panic disorder and phobia. The experience and the help that I received from a psychologist was so life-changing that it has proved to be part of the reason that I decided twenty-seven years ago to change careers and become a counsellor. Some years later I took the decision to undergo more specific training in order to could practise as a psychoanalytic psychotherapist. It is particularly challenging for any of us as mental health professionals when a client presents with symptoms of full-blown panic attacks and phobia because such symptoms can be deep-seated. However, as I suffered such symptoms myself, I endeavour in this book to take a truly empathic approach towards how we should offer help to those clients presenting with panic and phobia. This book offers a specific way of offering help to clients that I have not encountered in any detail in any other published text I have been able to find among my travails.

I found that the method of treatment that I underwent with the help of a newly qualified clinical psychologist in the early 1970s was so beneficial that I am anxious for many others to be able to have this resource at their disposal too. Fortunately, I fell ill when NHS provision for mental health problems was far more generous than it is in today's climate of recession, when the resources available for mental health issues are far more stretched and do not receive the same prioritisation. I was introduced to a programme known as *systematic desensitisation*, and I assiduously dedicated myself to it for several months to aid my recovery. I was rewarded for my efforts by a full recovery that has enabled me to live a normal, carefree life for the past forty-two years. I feel fortunate and grateful that I have, since the treatment, been able to live a fulfilling life, and have never suffered a relapse to those years that were literally filled with fear.

In my early twenties, my qualifications meant that I was bound for a career in marketing, but I became so ill with agoraphobia that I was unable to put my theoretical knowledge gained at college to any use as I was unable to function in the workplace. The systematic desensitisation programme introduced to me by my psychologist enabled me to move on and to start living normally again. I was able to realise my ambition to work in paid employment and enjoy a career in marketing, before starting a family two years later. After being a full-time mother for a decade, I remained so grateful for the help I had received from a mental health professional that I felt intensely motivated to change my career path and to start to train for an entirely different career—as a counsellor and then as a psychotherapist.

During the past three decades, I have helped numerous individuals suffering from panic, phobia, and diffuse anxiety states to find a way out of the "prison" that takes over their life when they become struck down by panic. It is common for sufferers to adopt the strategy of avoidance, and to make all sorts of detailed plans and excuses to avoid situations that raise feelings of anxiety and panic. As a consequence, their day-to-day existence is reduced to a mere "half-life", and they become unfulfilled and sad because they can no longer take part in what most of the population take for granted as normal living.

In the book, there are two chapters that present extended case studies of individuals who have surmounted the anxiety and panic that had taken over their lives. One of these case studies tells the story of recovery from severe agoraphobia (which resonates to my own experience), while the other tells the story of a client who came to me because she was suffering from driving phobia. Shorter case examples of other courageous individuals with whom I have worked can be found throughout the chapters in this book. Also, as a supervisor of other counsellors, I have also taught this method of overcoming panic and phobia to a good number of supervisees: counsellors who have utilised my expertise to oversee their work and as a resource for learning new skills.

The book aims to put forward to you a way of tackling panic disorder and phobia by showing you how to help clients by working through a systematic desensitisation programme. This method will be explained very clearly in Chapters Six and Seven, with extended case examples in Chapters Eight and Nine. These two case studies describe step-by-step just how this method was put into practice by two individuals with my help and encouragement as their therapist. It is sadly true that in the present day where financial provision is stretched to breaking point in the NHS, there are few resources allocated to mental health issues. The changing ideology that was born as a result of the backlash against abuse occurring in the old asylums and mental hospitals led to the birth of the era of "care in the community" in the late 1970s. It was felt that there would be less opportunity for abuse of patients, and less of a stigma in mental illness, if help was provided in day centres, hostels, sheltered housing, and care at home. This was accompanied by the rationale that individuals can be treated more effectively within their home environment than in a hospital setting. This became, and has remained, the dominant ideology. As many of you may have grown to suspect, there was an underlying financial motivation beneath the political rhetoric. "Care in the community" does not require the same vast amounts of investment, either in terms of infrastructure or the sheer multitude of personnel that were involved in the provision of the asylums and mental hospitals. For an excellent personal account of help that could be accessed in those days in the "asylum era", I suggest you read Barbara Taylor's autobiographical account of how she personally was helped by an analyst for two decades in *The Last Asylum: A Memoir of Madness in our Times* (Taylor, 2015). It provides an interesting insight into both her personal experience as an inpatient and as an outpatient at Friern Hospital in London, and is also written from her perspective as an historian. Friern Hospital was one of the last asylums to be closed the 1990s, and the book consists of a fascinating tale of her journey through what she herself terms as "madness" and the beneficial effects that she experienced from long-term psychotherapeutic help.

On a positive note, however, the death of the asylums and large scale mental hospitals has enabled mental health issues to be spoken about more openly, because the subject is now less constrained by the pejorative connotations associated with it during the "asylum era". Strides still need to be made, however, as there remain, regrettably, feelings of shame and guilt that accompany mental illness, which is in sharp contrast to the attitude to physical illness, such as cancer or a broken leg. Any of us individuals who have suffered from long-term mental illness will be aware of the deficit comparison of mental illness as compared to physical illness, and the accompanying lack of resources given to it by successive governments. However, it is also happily true to say that this negative connotation is far less marked than it was forty years ago when I suffered from agoraphobia during my twenties. Primarily, the change that is continuing to evolve is due to the courage of affected individuals who have been honest and courageous enough to speak out and talk about their experiences. I hope that I can add to that impetus by writing this book.

However, it is also unfortunately true that resources to help those with mental health issues have declined drastically in the past thirty years. My younger daughter has suffered from mental illness for the past twenty years, but it has been impossible to access help for her mental health issues from the NHS during that period of time. It is only five years since she was finally diagnosed with bipolar disorder, because despite my fight for recognition, her plight was ignored. Diagnosis (incidentally by a psychiatrist accessed through private resources) has made a considerable difference to her life, since she now receives appropriate medication to combat the recurring symptoms of episodes of mania and overwhelming depression. No help has been forthcoming during those two decades from the NHS apart from the much-valued and appreciated support of her dedicated GP. We have been forced to spend hard-earned cash upon accessing treatment from a psychiatrist and counsellors within the private sector. Others may well not be able to make this choice.

The purpose of this book is not to make a deliberate political statement about the NHS provision of care for those who are mentally ill. Nevertheless, the fact that resources in the NHS are scarce does constitute one of my major motivations in writing this book. I aim to help you to help your clients—you may work in the NHS yourself or alternatively in the burgeoning private sector of counsellors, psychotherapists, psychologists, or psychiatrists. This book puts forward a method that you can apply in your own work, and from which you have every chance of helping to free your clients from the symptoms of panic and phobia. Some readers may also find their way to this resource as sufferers of panic and phobia themselves, and for them I have included Chapter Twelve on the sourcing of help through private provision.

Before I move on to describe the systematic desensitisation programme, I feel it is useful if I talk in the first few chapters about the sorts of behaviour, cognitions, and feelings associated with anxiety, panic disorder, and phobia. I will also talk about the development of phobias, and will describe a number of the more common phobias from which individuals suffer. It may sound incredible but the truth is that many individuals who find their way to your consulting rooms do not at that stage recognise that it is appropriate for them to have a clinical diagnosis of panic disorder or phobia. This is particularly true if the disorder has developed gradually over a period of time. I find that clients can be greatly relieved to be given a label to describe the way they are feeling at this particular time in their life, and to realise that they are not alone in suffering this way. A diagnosis of a mental health problem, while often shocking, provides a way forward to recovery that they have not been able to access until diagnosis. It can prove a way out of a recurring nightmare in which they feel trapped. Alternatively, the symptoms may have struck them so suddenly, that they are at present reeling from the shock of the loss of their "normal way of living". You are no doubt aware that many such clients secretly harbour the fear that they are "going mad" or "insane". However, I have met so many clients who have been too scared to voice this to anyone, particularly to their GP, or even to their "nearest and dearest". This will have led to your clients feeling increasingly isolated, and this in turn increases the vicious circle of pain, frustration, and fear. I have found that many clients are so wrapped in their own bubble of confusing and overriding, difficult-to-bear feelings, that they are convinced that something dreadful is happening. Perhaps the thought crosses their mind: "Am I suffering from a heart attack?" or "I must be dying". In fact, these thoughts are part of what I personally describe as "a feeling of unreality". This is known technically as "derealisation" and "depersonalisation". These are very real thoughts and feelings, which mean that the sufferer no longer feels in touch or a part of the every-day world.

Individuals have expressed to me how nothing in their life seems simple any longer; all aspects of their life may appear to be difficult because of unwelcome complications. For example, they may ask themselves the following question: "How can I go to that theatre visit to see a play unless I can be sure that I can get out quickly? I must be able to sit by the aisle, and perhaps those seats won't be free!" This book aims first of all to help you to recognise the myriad of symptoms that anxiety can and, indeed, does cause, and thus will help you to be able to pick up the clues of an underlying anxiety disorder from what may seem like a "throwaway comment" by a client. As therapists, we really act as detectives in many of our sessions, teasing out the truth from our clients' seemingly innocent comments that, if their significance is recognised, tell us about an individual's psychopathology.

Chapter Four labels the particular sorts of anxiety disorder and phobia in case you are not conversant with the cluster of symptoms that each contains. Is it post-traumatic stress disorder (PTSD), obsessive compulsive disorder (OCD), generalised anxiety disorder (GAD), or is your client suffering from a phobia such as agoraphobia, social phobia, or claustrophobia? Or maybe they are suffering from a combination of phobias; in fact, this is a common occurrence.

The book will also explain how anxiety symptoms differ from panic: when is it that the problem escalates to the more intense level of discomfort and distress that panic attacks involve? Is the development of a phobia a logical extension of frequent panic attacks? Before going on to talk about the systematic desensitisation programme, I will look at the way we need to start to systematically recognise—at a conscious level—the myriad of symptoms that our clients may be suffering, and the situations that they have become accustomed to avoid. In fact, a range of symptoms often seem to present in such a confusing and upsetting clutch—it is understandably hard for individuals to accept that all these symptoms are really caused by one problem: profound anxiety.

I hope it will help you to be able to tell your client about what is known as the flight or fight response (Chapter Two). This response, in fact, comes as a result of the hormones, adrenaline, noradrenaline, and cortisol, rushing round our bodies, causing chaos.

The central purpose of this book, however, is to provide you with a specific way of tackling your clients' anxiety, panic, or phobia. This is known as a systematic desensitisation programme. I will provide a detailed description of how to tackle phobia and persistent anxiety that enables you to help your clients to rid themselves of the terrors of their syndrome. It will provide you with the tools to deal with any similar symptoms with which anyone may present in your consulting room at any time in your career as a mental health professional, now or at some time in the future.

In Chapters Six and Seven, I will provide a detailed description of how to engage clients in a systematic desensitisation programme. This programme is based upon the proven fact that while *avoiding* stressful and panic-producing circumstances may be effective in lessening distressing symptoms in the short-term, it is *never* helpful in the long-term because it reduces the choices in their life dramatically, and prevents clients from participating in life to the full. They are then inclined to develop other mental health problems such as depression and suicidal ideation.

At this stage, I will just outline the concepts that you will meet in working through a systematic desensitisation programme. It is actually a very straightforward series of exercises that you teach your client to undertake in a specific order, while walking alongside them to offer encouragement and a sense of purpose. Essentially, it enables your clients to get out of the habit of taking avoidance strategies to manage life, and instead provides them with the tools to *gradually expose themselves* to the situations that they find stressful. I will say at this point, however, that this method of overcoming anxiety and panic needs to be worked on, consciously, and with determination, by both you as the therapist and by your clients. It requires you to work consistently towards motivating your clients to work at this programme for a sustained period of time. There are no quick fixes. It is most likely that it has taken some time for your clients to develop these fears and anxieties; as such, it is therefore expectable that it will take persistent effort to achieve a cure for their panic and/or phobia. You may like to use the dictum: "You get out of life what you put in!" One of the watchwords of the programme is repetition of the words: practice, practice, practice. This is the only way to help your client to "cure" themselves of the "bad" habits that they have developed—perfectly understandable, and not a quality by which to judge anyone— but now you have to explain that they need to adopt a new and proactive way of life. You need to explain that they are "bad" habits because these habits do not serve them well; not that you are calling them a "bad" person in any way (as would be meant if you were implying that they were "evil" or "cruel"). You need to stress that it will feel strange at first for them to learn to act differently, just as any new way of tackling something is strange at the beginning of change. But above all, they need to get rid of the "bad" habits and replace them with "good" habits. This takes practice and repetition of various procedures, in order to build confidence, of which they are capable with your support.

Essentially, a systematic desensitisation programme involves you first of all teaching a programme of *relaxation*. It needs to be said that this will take each of your clients several weeks to master, by practising the exercises assiduously at least twice per day. It is important that you stress this and help to motivate them. However, once having mastered the skills of progressive relaxation, they will not only be ready to move on to the challenges of the next part of recovery, but also they will have a skill useful at all sorts of times of their future life (to use before job interviews, presentations, or at times of being unable to sleep). While you are teaching the art of relaxation, I suggest you use some of the time during sessions to help your client to think about and identify the sort of situations or circumstances that make them feel anxious or panicky. These ideas will be used to build "a hierarchy" consisting of some of these situations. Building a hierarchy entails you constructing, together with your clients, a list of tasks that they are going to carry out, which gradually increase in terms of difficulty. The tasks are numbered from one to ten. At this stage, each number represents a task that at the moment your clients may personally find difficult to imagine daring to complete as you devise the hierarchy together. Task One represents a task that they may still be a part of their daily life (although it leaves them feeling anxious), or that they have undertaken in the recent past with only a little difficulty. For example, an individual suffering from agoraphobia, and who has not been outside the house for several years, may choose with her therapist to set herself the task of walking out of the front door and down the front path of her garden as far as the street. You will be instrumental in helping your clients to practise each task a number of times, before moving on to the next task. Gradually, together, you work up the hierarchy, choosing to move on, one by one, to other situations that the clients will find a little more challenging than the previous one, until at Task Ten they will be able to achieve the situation that they most dread at the moment. In effect, the programme consists of a series of "graded stepping stones".

It is a good idea to work out the hierarchy on a piece of paper, so that you can amend it and alter it until you have honed it to be totally appropriate for your particular client. This should be a collaborative effort. You then begin the job of helping your clients to actually accomplish the tasks in reality; this involves a gradual participation in a number of different situations. With regard to teaching the accomplishment of Task One: you first organise that the client gets into a relaxed state of mind and body, using the "tense then let go" exercises that I outline in Chapter Six. Once feeling relaxed, you can help the client (in the consulting room) to *visualise* taking part in the task. You help them to build a mental picture of all the steps that this task will involve, thinking carefully about the precise details that completion of the task entails. You may then persuade them to repeat this visualisation for several days at home while in a relaxed state of mind; then you arrange with them that they will choose to make a certain day "a D-Day". After having completed the relaxation exercises, they will first of all visualise the task and then go out and set about *completing the task* in the real world. You need to help them to develop the ability to relax again and reduce their agitation when they become anxious during this process.

It is helpful to recognise at this stage that your clients' progress will not be a story of absolute success. They will encounter difficulties, so the next stage is to analyse with them at a succeeding session, how accomplishing the task actually affected them—you need to identify what parts were "easy" and which parts were "difficult". You need to help them to think how they might eliminate these setbacks when they undertake the task again. This is all a part of what is termed *the review*.

You help your clients by giving encouragement and words of advice, to work through each of the tasks from one to ten, suggesting that they practise each task several times to build self-confidence, until they feel ready to move on to the next task.

There are three sets of "watchwords" or phrases that you need to employ when taking clients through this programme: the first is: practice, practice, practice. The second idea that you need to instil is: Take the time to master the relaxation exercises. Third, you need to teach your clients the following adage: Do not judge yourself. You need to make it clear that this is not a competition—expect to encounter setbacks, but do not be downhearted: your clients *will* move in a forward direction to a new phase of their lives where they will be able to celebrate the cessation of a life full of worry about situations that have, for a while, caused much conflict in their minds and bodies.

This is a well-proven path to recovery from phobia and panic disorder that may well have been crippling your clients' lives for some time. I know—I was introduced to this method myself as a patient in my twenties, to rid me of the totally overwhelming symptoms of agoraphobia. As I have already mentioned, the case studies in Chapters Eight and Nine, provide you with examples of how in my turn as a therapist I have helped clients suffering from differing phobias to overcome their debilitating symptoms.

Later in the book, I will also address a number of cognitive strategies that you might like to adopt in order to deal with your clients' anxiety symptoms, and reduce them to manageable proportions. This includes various cognitive techniques such as the challenging of the "negative self-talk" that unconsciously give rise to anxious feelings. It helps your clients to be able to start to recognise that they are employing particular ways of "skewed" thinking; for instance, there is often a tendency to "catastrophise": to take what is only a possibility and make of it a reality, as if it had already actually happened. We may recognise that our clients are prone to what I term "black and white thinking"; never seeing that life is actually lived in shades of grey, without always being experienced in extremes. We may analyse that our clients may have got into a habit of always looking at the negatives, and of disregarding the positives: of being pessimistic rather than optimistic. It is also common for individuals suffering from anxiety to be their own worst critic, continuously resorting to self-blame and self-criticism. In other words, they may be their own worst enemy.

I am an integrative psychotherapist, despite having undertaken a psychoanalytic training. However, I find that although this systematic desensitisation programme is essentially a behavioural programme, it is immensely useful in cases of panic disorder and phobia. However, as I have outlined above, I combine this with the use of cognitive strategies to help my clients achieve their recovery. It helps to use cognitive techniques to circumnavigate the obstacles that they will probably encounter on the journey back to health. I also find that it is helpful to employ some psychodynamic techniques using a brief-model of psychodynamic counselling. In this way, you can enable your clients to briefly explore their life history. This is suggested so that you can help your clients to find the underlying factors that explain why their phobias first developed. Clients often find it deeply satisfying and reassuring to have found an answer to "the why question". With your training, you can help them to work through significant events in their childhood and adolescence, and to make links between what occurred and the way they are tortured by symptoms now. It may well be that at first they only have a sketchy memory of some event or feeling that endured, or alternatively they may not have understood the significance of the event way back in their life at the time. Once you are armed with this information, you will then have an opportunity to help your clients to change their habitual response to anxiety-provoking situations in the "here and now" of the present. It may well be that the old ways of dealing with the problem are now outmoded and no longer provide a productive way of living, and you can encourage them to change their ways of thinking, feeling, and behaving. More will be said on using psychodynamic techniques alongside the behavioural programme to facilitate a complete recovery.

The book concludes with an overview of the topics covered, and a hope that by using this book to help your clients, you will enable them to find a new, more fulfilling way to live life. Essentially, this book puts forward an integrative approach to the task of helping those who present to us with panic disorder and phobia.

To avoid the somewhat clumsy conventions of s/he, her/his, throughout this volume I have employed the female pronoun when discussing the patient or person suffering from phobia, anxiety, and/or panic attacks. Of course, men also suffer from these conditions, and all the exercises and suggestions are equally relevant to male clients. Also, I have tended to use the male pronoun when talking about medical practitioners, although many are in actual fact female.

I take great pleasure in dedicating this book to Anne, the clinical psychologist who led me through a process of recovery from severe agoraphobia when I was in my early twenties. I thank you, Anne, with all my heart, for had it not been for your help, I might never have achieved my years as a practising psychotherapist, and my more recent career as an author.

CHAPTER ONE

The symptoms of anxiety and fear

Anxiety and fear

It is absolutely true that anxiety and fear, in reasonable amounts, are a normal part of everyone's life. It is usual, and expectable, that when we are faced with sitting an examination, or attending a job interview, or asking the boss for a pay rise, or finding our way across London for the first time, the majority of us will suffer *some level of anxiety*. Similarly, if we are faced with being in our home while an earthquake or a tornado is in progress, or we have just been involved in a serious car accident, then it is to be expected that we will experience feelings of fear.

However, I have placed the words "some level of anxiety" in italics in the above paragraph because this highlights the central point. In the case of your clients, do the feelings of anxiety or fear wash over them during the event, but pass when the situation is over? Are there logical reasons to explain why they are suffering from anxiety? Do the symptoms so commonly associated with anxiety (which I will describe in detail shortly) pass quite quickly, and enable them to return to feeling normal within a reasonable period of time? So— the point I am making is that feelings of anxiety and fearfulness are normal, *if* they are experienced in response to a definite, logical stimulus, and are not experienced in an out-of-control manner, or for an extended period.

For those clients who suffer from an excess of anxious feelings, or even experience feelings of naked fear, the anxiety is different in several sorts of ways:

- Your clients will frequently not be consciously aware of any particular stimulus that brings on the feelings of anxiety. They may well exclaim: "There seems to be no logical reason for me to feel the way I do."

- Your clients may tend to feel anxious for most of the day; it may well be that they only experience some relief in the safety of "home", but equally, even this environment may not make them feel at ease.

- They may well tend to express the uncomfortable belief that they fear that they are never going to return to "normal". Maybe they will declare that "I can't handle life nowadays" and may wonder, "Will these feelings ever go away again?"

- Most probably, they are presently finding it hard to concentrate and think clearly. They may use the expression: "My brain's in a fog!"

- They may be suffering from a fear that they have a serious health problem. "Am I having a heart attack?", "Do I have cancer?", "Am I developing some debilitating and deteriorating health condition such as multiple sclerosis or rheumatoid arthritis?", "What is the reason for that ache/pain/feeling that I keep suffering?"

- They may well arrive in your consulting room complaining that no-one has understood what they are going through; that no-one has taken them seriously. This thought may be accompanied by feelings of anger and resentment, that others are enjoying life while life is terrible for them.

- The thought may run through their heads from time to time that they are going mad or insane. It may take a little time before they trust you enough to confide in you regarding this fear.

- If they are suffering from an anxiety state, and more particularly from panic attacks, it is probable that they are plagued with a fear that they are going to die. It helps to explain that this is all a part of the feeling that is known as "derealisation": this involves a feeling of detachment from the real world, and a feeling that one is at the present time unable to think about things in a logical manner, or act in what they would consider a habitual way.

The common physical and emotional symptoms of anxiety

I hope it will be helpful if I list the common symptoms of anxiety below. Sometimes, clients present with difficulties but do not consciously recognise that they are suffering from a generalised anxiety state (GAD) or from a named phobia. Many clients have described experiencing panic attacks without being aware that this is actually a known syndrome. As therapists, we need to look out for the signs and signals that an individual is suffering from a clinical diagnosis of anxiety, help them to come to terms with such a diagnosis, and find a way out from what can be a form of "living hell".

Physical symptoms

Heart

Increased heart rate, often felt as palpitations; a feeling of "fluttering" in the chest or of a pounding heart; a client may describe a conscious awareness of their heart beating or that it seems "to skip a beat" every so often. Another complaint you may hear is that they register their pulse in their ears.

Pain

Chest pain or tightness; stomach ache or pain; headache; pain in the neck and/or shoulders; pain in the legs; dental pain (from teeth grinding). A client may describe a feeling of muscle tension in a certain part of their anatomy, or even throughout a whole range of different parts of the body.

Head

Constant and prolonged headache; migraine; dizziness; vertigo (a feeling of everything moving constantly; of being unsure of the edge of things); blurred vision; feeling of being unbalanced and maybe difficulty in walking in a straight line (ataxia); tinnitus (constant noises within the inner ear); abnormal sensitivity to light (photophobia);

abnormal sensitivity to noise (phonophobia); abnormal sensitivity to smell (osmophobia); dry mouth; difficulty in swallowing or chewing food; difficulty breathing (a sensation of being unable to catch their breath); numbness and/or tingling in some part(s) of the body.

Digestive problems

Irritable bowel syndrome (IBS); constipation; diarrhoea; indigestion; "burping"; passing a lot of wind (flatulence); pain in the gut and intestines.

Energy

Feeling of constant tiredness; lethargy; lassitude; exhaustion.

General practitioners report sometimes that up to half the patients that they see each day are suffering from psychological symptoms or psychosomatic disorders (O'Sullivan, 2015).

Cognitive symptoms of anxiety

- Difficulties in concentration, and in completing tasks (either at work or in the home).
- Decreased capacity to think creatively.
- Problems with memory loss.
- A definitive tendency to worry about anything and everything.
- Catastrophising (a tendency to "jump" in one's thoughts to the worst scenario possible, without having any evidence that this is really the case).
- Black and white thinking—not seeing things in shades of grey: instead there is a tendency to think and believe: "I must have . . .!"
- The repeated scanning of the body for signs of illness.
- Feelings of unreality: descriptions of not feeling they are really "here" with other people. I describe it from my own past experience as a feeling as if I were somehow "suspended above" everyone else, and was not able to fully take part in whatever was occurring. These feelings are technically known as depersonalisation and derealisation.
- Preoccupation with certain thoughts: these are known as "ruminations" repetitive, obsessive cognitive patterns.

Emotional symptoms of anxiety

- Increased irritability.
- Constant sense of fear.
- Lowered self-esteem.
- Lowered level of self-confidence.
- Fear of serious illness.
- Preoccupation with routine; doing things to a certain pattern or ritual accompanied with a compulsion to repeat the ritual if not carried out "correctly".
- Maintaining superstitious beliefs.
- Hoarding/collecting.
- Being overly concerned with staying safe.
- Self-medicating with increased alcohol, prescription or over-the-counter (OTC) medications, or illegal drugs such as ecstasy, cannabis, or heroin.
- Over-eating or avoidance of eating (anorexic tendencies; bulimia; bingeing; purging).
- Above all: avoidance of whatever constitutes "the dreaded situation" in the individual's mind.

I will return to the point that you may discern that your client is using avoidance as a main strategy in later chapters: it is central that you use your analytic skills to recognise that despite your client's protestations that they are following a logical path, they are taking avoidant action. Some clients can make use of very plausible arguments as to the reason they are behaving in a certain way. It is not that they are consciously seeking to deceive—this represents the use of the defence mechanism of denial in one of its most sophisticated forms; they are in fact deceiving themselves at an unconscious level. In Chapters Six, Seven, and Ten I will instruct you to help your clients to take steps to:

1. Recognise the use of the denial mechanism,
2. To escape from the "avoidance vicious circle" that they have unconsciously developed as a first-line response to deal with overwhelming anxiety.

In the early days of suffering from anxiety, it often seems that the only way that individuals can tolerate life is by avoidance of stressful situations. This answer may seem useful in the short-term, but over a longer period of time (as many of you will be aware) your client seeks to avoid an increasing range of stimuli until they become unable to take part in normal life whatsoever.

I remember all too well reaching this point in my life during my early twenties when I suffered from agoraphobia but had as yet not realised I was suffering from this phobia. I found a treatment plan in the systematic desensitisation programme that I grew to know very well with the help of a psychologist, and it enabled me to return to normal living for the remainder of my life. As a therapist I have used this method with many clients over the past three decades, with amazing results.

However, in order to achieve this end, you need to help your clients to gradually abandon the cycle of avoidance. Avoidance breeds increased fear, which in turn means more situations are avoided. This vicious circle continues to spiral out of control until the individual finds that their daily routine has shrunk so that they can only participate in a minimal number of activities. It may be when your client presents in the consulting room that she does not accept that she is deeply involved in this vicious circle. You need, of course, to use tact and careful language to offer challenge as a gift that your client finds palatable to hear and take in. It is then your task to help your client to change this vicious circle into a fruitful circle—where her horizons in life start to expand again. I will explain how this process can be gradually accomplished in Chapters Six and Seven.

But first, in Chapter Two, I am going to talk about the reasons that the anxious person suffers such a welter of symptoms. You may already be aware that most of the symptoms are a result of a range of physiological changes that take place in our bodies when we feel fearful. There is a simple reason for this complicated chain of symptoms, and I know that when I discovered this, I found it calming. When you explain this to your clients, they too may feel reassured and relieved.

CHAPTER TWO

The fight or flight cycle

The link between fear and anxiety

T here is a simple reason why we as individuals suffer the myriad of symptoms when we are anxious, and why these symptoms seem to multiply and grow more pronounced over time.

When we feel fear, our bodies are programmed, since primeval times, to release two hormones, adrenaline and noradrenaline. Our brains, in response to a fearful situation, send a biochemical message to our pituitary gland to release a hormone that in turn triggers the adrenal gland to release the hormones that I have just mentioned.

Now, your clients may well be wondering why as human beings we are flooded with what seem to be inconvenient and unnecessary hormones that are in reality causing such havoc in their lives at present. In fact, these two hormones have a very important function. We need to think back to Stone Age Man. When he was faced by a fearful situation—say the approach of a bear that was intending to eat him to slake his hunger, or he came upon an ambush of rival tribesmen—he needed to take action very quickly in order to save his own life. There were two options open to him at this point: fight or flight. He could either prepare himself in an instant to fight "the enemy" (be it a bear or rival tribesmen) or alternatively, he needed the energy to run away as fast as his legs could carry him.

This is what is known as: the fight or flight response.

It is very important that you understand this mechanism and explain it clearly to your clients because it will help them to understand why they are suffering from the myriads of symptoms that are troubling them at this time in their lives.

In short, the adrenaline that pulsed round Stone Age Man's body at this point performs a number of functions for the human being in today's society:

- Breathing becomes faster and shallower, thus supplying more oxygen to one's muscles, which in turn provides increased levels of energy. This enabled Stone Age Man to run away faster, or have more strength with which to fight the enemy. However, in the present day, for the person suffering an anxiety state, who does not need literally to run away or fight, the effect of this increased oxygen explains a number of symptoms. For example, the increased oxygen leads to feelings of light-headedness; it blurs vision; it results in breathlessness. In fact, your client may well be hyperventilating. This occurs when any of us breathe in such a way—more shallowly and at a faster rate—because this effects the ratio of oxygen to carbon dioxide in our systems. The answer for the person who is hyperventilating is to breathe slowly into a paper bag (it is important to stress the use of a paper bag not a plastic one for safety reasons). This effectively enables the individual to inhale a higher concentration of carbon dioxide, and this rectifies the ratio of oxygen to carbon dioxide in the bloodstream.

- The adrenaline makes the heart beat faster, so that blood is driven to one's brain and limbs. Again, this was very useful for Stone Age Man. With more blood flow to the brain, he was able to think faster: he literally needed to think on his feet in this situation. Ability to think fast and make quick decisions may have enabled him to continue to survive. For this reason, an increased supply to his limbs enabled him to run away, or engage in a battle of the fists, more readily and easily. But for the person suffering anxiety in today's world, this response leaves them with palpitations, chest pains, and a tingling or slightly numb feeling all over. This again explains a whole raft of symptoms: again, these symptoms are the result of that hormone, adrenaline.

- As the blood was needed by Stone Age Man in his brain and his limbs, it was therefore diverted from his digestive system. No-one about to fight a war is planning to stop and eat a gargantuan meal first. Thus, temporarily, blood is not required in the digestive system. Therefore, if your client is suffering from an anxiety state, they tend to feel sick or nauseous, suffering from indigestion or stomach cramps. Over time, as a person gets accustomed to the fight or flight mechanism, the individual may develop irritable bowel syndrome (IBS).
- In tandem with the above, the liver releases stored sugar to provide fuel so that Stone Age Man had more energy with which to fight. You will be growing accustomed by now to my argument—your client does not need the excess energy that a caveman needed, and therefore this increases the symptoms of indigestion.
- Sphincter muscles at the openings of the bladder and anus become relaxed. This was to enable Stone Age Man to evacuate the urine and faeces in order to allow him to run away or fight more effectively. It is for this reason that an individual will tend to "wet" or "soil" herself when she is afraid. It explains why your client may have the urge to urinate frequently, or to empty her bowels: to get to a toilet as a matter of urgency. It also helps to explain stomach cramps and aches and pains.
- Stone Age Man was hot from all this sudden and unexpected exercise. The adrenaline had caused him to perspire. Your clients, too, may frequently describe how they become drenched in sweat when suffering acute anxiety.

Thus, you can see from the above description, the various effects of the release of adrenaline. This explains how many anxiety symptoms result directly from adrenaline coursing through the body.

You can also gather from my description of Stone Age Man's trials that the release of adrenaline was very useful for him. Similarly, if *we* are truly faced with a really frightening scenario—say a tsunami suddenly hit our village—we, too, would need to have the effects of the adrenaline in order to make our getaway and to think fast, on the move. So you can explain that anxiety and fear are very necessary mechanisms and feelings to experience at times because they enable us to cope well in situations of danger. Adrenaline is fine if it is released in response to a situation that provokes a valid reason to feel fearful.

The problem arises, however, when individuals become fearful and there is no logical reason to feel this way. If they were able to think and feel rationally it would mean that their hormones would not set off the fight or flight chain of reactions. It may be true to say for those of your clients who are suffering from a generalised anxiety disorder (GAD) that the daily round of situations they face is sufficient to set off these chains of events. They then tend to hold on to that anxiety for longer than necessary or normal. Contrary to this, a person with a normal response to an anxiety-arousing situation will soon return to feeling relaxed, in contrast to the individual suffering an anxiety state who remains anxious for a protracted period of hours or days on end. In the latter case, the adrenaline floods through the body, and the individual suffers the various symptoms as a result of an overdose of the hormone.

Eventually, however, the adrenal glands—responsible for the release of adrenaline—get tired and stop producing adrenaline. They literally run out of energy. This is the reason that everyone stops feeling anxious and, temporarily at least, lose the palpitations and feelings of unreality.

Fear is a direct, focused response to a specific event. We are consciously aware of feeling *fear*.

Anxiety on the other hand is often a feeling that individuals do not consciously acknowledge or give a label to when they start to feel this way. Once we encourage our clients to recognise it, we can help them to use their memory, intelligence, and imagination to think their response through, and to decide whether it is appropriate to feel anxious or not. For most of us, for most of our lives, we are able to do this, but sometimes, maybe because of a specific event or trauma (a trigger) the individual has effectively learned, over the ensuing period of time, a "bad" habit ("bad" in the sense of being unproductive and uncomfortable, not "bad" meaning "evil"). This book sets out to tell you a systematic way of helping your clients to unlearn the "bad" habit of prolonged periods of anxiety and "relearn" a productive, healthy, and happy way to live life.

A psychodynamic perspective:
how and why do clients' anxiety symptoms perpetuate?

First of all, in the case of many clients we are capable of uncovering how some experience of trauma or acutely anxious period of life precipitated the development of the client's anxiety state. Often, clients can find it illuminating, and gain a real palpable sense of relief, by being able to work out what situation occurred in the past that led to the development of their anxiety state. It is useful to know the nature of the original *trigger*.

For this reason, when I am working as a psychotherapist with individuals suffering from a generalised anxiety disorder or phobia, it has become my practice to adopt *a two-pronged approach*, and thus I suggest you adopt this approach too. By this, I mean that I employ both *cognitive behavioural* techniques and *psychodynamic* techniques in an integrative way. First, the cognitive behavioural techniques that I describe later in this book are capable by themselves of providing the incredible benefit of giving us a way in which we can enable individuals to "unlearn" the "bad" habits of their fight or flight cycle of anxiety, which have come into play as a direct result of the adrenaline pouring round their bodies for a sustained period of time. A systematic desensitisation programme enables us to teach our clients to relax when faced with one of the events that trigger this anxiety-response, and to face the feared event or situation in a calm and relaxed manner. Learning this programme enables the client to remain calm and relaxed, and effectively breaks "the fear of the fear" cycle. In so doing, the adrenaline stops flowing.

Second, at the same time as I teach individual clients the skills of a systematic desensitisation programme (a behavioural intervention), I also lead the client through a *psychodynamic* voyage of discovery. Whether or not you are trained in a psychodynamic modality, what you are nevertheless capable of doing is to talk to your clients about the past in a structured way, leading them gently through a process of recalling significant events from their childhood, adolescence, and recent past. It is almost always possible to analyse the clues that they will provide and reach an answer to the conundrum of why an individual has developed an anxious way of thinking and behaving. Frequently, you will find that an individual is unconsciously "remembering" a traumatic event that is at the root of their personal "anxiety-cycle". Memories of this precipitating trauma, or the first experience of a panic attack (which is always quite terrifying), keeps reoccurring in the individual's unconscious mind. Put simply, the thought passes through the mind so quickly that the individual does not consciously recognise that they have encountered thoughts of this event from the past. I find it helpful to explain the way this works by using the analogy of what was known in the 1960s as "subliminal advertising". Advertisements on television were invented to be flashed upon the television screen so briefly that the viewer did not consciously appreciate that they had been subjected to the image, say, of a particular washing powder. However, the repeated images of this particular washing powder entered the individual's unconscious mind, and this effectively predisposed the individual to buy that particular brand of washing powder when next faced with an array of washing powders on the supermarket shelves. I am sure that you will not be surprised to be told that this sort of advertising, once investigated by the Advertising Standards Authority (ASA), was decreed as unethical and manipulative of our unconscious processes, and was thus banned from use. However, I am describing the mechanism used in subliminal advertising because it draws a parallel, and shows how these intrusive unconscious memories of the original trigger event or fearful situation play in the client's mind—subliminally—without their consciously being able to identify them.

Using psychodynamic techniques, you can help your client to become consciously aware of what has hitherto been unconscious. You will then be able to help the client to appreciate that incidents in the past may well be having a seminal effect upon them in today's world. As a therapist, once they recognise their particular trigger, you can then help your client to change the way she responds to the triggering factor. It usually needs to be fully explained that while this was the only possible way to react to the original event, this mechanism for dealing with the stressor is no longer a useful way of thinking and behaving in the present. Again, you need to help them unlearn the unproductive way of reacting and replace this with a productive way of behaving and feeling.

It is usually a reality that the individual had no choice in the way she dealt with the situation at the time it occurred. For example, the trigger may have been the repeated bullying behaviour of another pupil in their class while they were at primary school. Now, at the time, they may have been a defenceless eight-year-old, who would have been enforced, by the law of the land and well-meaning parents, to attend school every day. As they were only eight years old, it is most unlikely that they were capable of defending themselves assertively with the bully. Also, it is most likely that they lacked the verbal acuity to articulate their feelings, or describe the nature of the abuse, to parents or loved ones. Friends probably did not understand or were not aware, and in any case, were not mature enough to help in their plight. So they were rendered defenceless. This is not the case now that they are an adult of say, forty-five years of age. They may be suffering an echo of that original abuse at the hands of a colleague in the workplace. With this hypothetical personal history, the individual client will be hypersensitive about bullying behaviour because of the original event when eight years old. However, the current behaviour of their work colleague, (say), will remind them unconsciously of the original bullying, and their innate inability to defend or extricate themselves from the situation when a youngster. Consequently, they begin to feel anxious every day in the mornings as they set off for work. In this way, they have developed the "bad" habit of feeling highly anxious and so the adrenaline pours round the body. However, until you adopt my two-pronged approach they may be unaware of the nature of the original trigger. As a therapist, you are capable of unlocking the original memories and then to help them to reassess their adult response to the stimulus. As I have said, your client may well have not been in a position to defend herself or to take avoidant action when aged eight, but the forty-five-year-old is in a different position. She can speak up assertively for herself; she can go and enlist the help of her boss or HR department; she can leave her current employment. The forty-five-year-old has choices. These were not available to her at age eight. Thus, you can help your client to reframe her original experience with the advantages of maturity, and create a different scenario using a psychodynamic format.

In the next chapter, we will look at the various thoughts and behaviours that our clients may have developed that in effect perpetuate, or even cause, the "anxiety-cycle" to develop and become a "bad habit".

CHAPTER THREE

What is the fear of the fear cycle and how is it maintained?

Physical reactions

In the preceding chapter I have detailed the changes that occur as a result of adrenaline coursing round the body. For example, a person may develop muscle tension in the legs, chest, and/or abdomen. For similar reasons associated with an excess of adrenaline, the individual may suffer breathlessness, dizziness, or palpitations. Any of these symptoms can be wrongly attributed to a serious, life-threatening health problem. Our clients may even have the thought: "I think I'm having a heart attack!" or "These are the symptoms of a stroke!", or "I've got bowel cancer and may die!" Alternatively, our clients may feel fearful in the "here and now"—they may feel highly embarrassed and out of control at the idea that they may unavoidably vomit in public, or faint, or lose control of bowel or bladder.

When I was twenty-one, I developed a profound fear of vomiting in public, and as a consequence I gradually stopped going out in case I fell ill and vomited in public, and I also feared that I might faint. In consequence, over a period of two years, I developed a severe compulsion to avoid going out—in reality, my "vomit phobia" morphed into full-blown agoraphobia (the fear of public spaces). Unconsciously, I had taken the decision that if I were to avoid going out in public, I would not embarrass myself by being taken ill suddenly. I did not make the connections at age twenty-one, and in the 1960s, few GP's had any real skills in dealing with mental health issues. I was prescribed tranquillisers and left to cope as best I could. I carried on with life, incrementally avoiding more and more of normal living. I had finished higher education at polytechnic, but felt totally unable to force myself to further my career by seeking a job. I dare not step outside the door. The "low-point" or crisis arrived when my husband was promoted and we moved geographical area, far away from my support network of family and friends. I realised, as it became increasingly difficult to even go out of the house to take my dog for a walk, that I had been reduced to living what I termed "a half-life". I was then aged twenty-three—hardly a stimulating way to live, and it was causing conflict in my marriage. Through sheer determination and desperation, I managed to access a psychologist who introduced me to a systematic desensitisation programme (as I describe in Chapters Six and Seven). Over the following six months, I gradually returned to being able to live normally. I felt well enough to apply for a job and go to work daily for the next two years. Then, my husband and I were confident enough in my recovery to decide to try for a baby. The systematic desensitisation programme revolutionised my life.

Some years later, my journey through this illness motivated me to choose to change career and start to train as a counsellor. During the course of psychotherapy, I came to understand the nature of my personal trigger. Personally, maybe because I have since become a psychoanalytic psychotherapist, or maybe because I simply have always liked to "know why", I found it very satisfying to understand the root of my troubles. First, it satisfied my curiosity and alleviated a sense of guilt and remorse. Second, it also enabled me to rationalise that I now had different capacities to deal with life-events than when I was an abused child, and that now, as an adult, I possessed the choice to react differently from that defenceless child. I have outlined above my personal fear-of-the-fear cycle. Now, I want to talk about the ways that individuals unconsciously maintain their fear of the fear cycles.

> Our clients suffer a physiological reaction to anxiety, and then the cycle repeats because each day they start to fear that the anxious symptoms will beset them again. The vicious circle of the fear of the fear is set in motion and spirals out of control.

I use as an example of the above vicious circle the knock-on effect of an individual suffering their first panic attack. This attack tends to have such a traumatic effect that the individual starts to fear that they will suffer a repetition of the experience. They are then inclined to avoid similar situations to the one when the first panic attack occurred. It is then that the fear of the fear cycle of anxiety starts to spiral out of control.

It is also likely that as a result of high anxiety levels, your client will begin to experience disturbed sleep patterns. Then, as they start to suffer the effects of sleep deprivation, stress levels increase generally. Again, the fear of the fear cycle cuts in and takes over the person's life.

Psychological mechanisms that maintain fear of the fear cycles

Anyone can suffer from biased patterns of thinking, and this presents itself in a number of dysfunctional ways:

- Selective attention: focusing upon "glass half empty": a pessimistic view of life, rather than looking from a optimistic perspective: "glass half full".
- self-reproach: this leads to the perpetuation of low self-esteem
- over-analysing and constant worrying
- black and white thinking
- catastrophising.

I will talk about each of these skewed ways of thinking in turn.

Selective attention: taking a pessimistic view on life

In this scenario, there is a tendency by the individual to exaggerate her expectations in life. For example, she may say: "Why does nothing ever go right for me? I am so much more unlucky than everyone else I know". This tendency is associated with the way some individuals perceive themselves as "victims". It is quite possible that this may be the result of the dominant world view that was held in the family of origin. There is a tendency in such families to focus upon what has gone wrong, rather than looking at life from an optimistic stance and concentrating on counting the family's blessings.

Associated with this "victim" approach to life is a tendency to over-generalise. One bad thing happens, and this is followed by the certainty that this is typical of life in general, and that this pattern of bad luck will repeat.

It is sometimes the case that such individuals will develop the habit of repeatedly "scanning their bodies" for signs of illness. I remember having a client who insisted that her husband scan her body in minute detail every week for signs of skin cancer. Now, it is wise to ask someone with whom you are intimate to scan your body from time to time—say, every three months—to check for new moles or mutations in any existing moles. But this sometimes becomes an obsession for an individual, who may also tend to cover themselves copiously in sun-cream before venturing outside for five minutes to feed the guinea pig in the garden. It is the received wisdom in today's society that we should all utilise the benefit of fifteen minutes in the sun every day (when it shines in England!) in order to avoid Vitamin D deficiency. Such individuals tend to ignore this dictum, in the fear that they will suffer skin cancer. You may become aware that such clients have a tendency "to check their body for signs of illness" several times per day. They may check their bodies literally, or run through a "list" mentally. They may become unnaturally aware of their bodily processes (e.g., peristalsis).

Self-reproach: lowered self-esteem

Frequently, you may have a growing awareness that a client is suffering from low self-esteem. A typical example is the person who returning from a holiday in Spain, having found it was not an overwhelming success, is certain that it is all her fault that the family did not enjoy the break more fully. In fact, they are no more responsible than several of their family members, or it may be that the booking information was misleading. Alternatively, in reality it may be no-one's fault: it may just be a twist of fate.

There is an associated tendency in such individuals to blame and to criticise themselves. As therapists, we need to teach our clients to show themselves the same level of kindness, consideration, and tolerance that they would most likely give to others. They need to be told firmly that they would not be wise to stay friends with a best friend who repeatedly says, "Oh, how stupidly you behaved today."

However, this is what they say to themselves. I have learned to stress the following mantra:

"Be kind to yourself".

Over-analysing and constant worrying

As a qualified psychoanalytic psychotherapist, I have learned to analyse as an integral part of my daily life, sitting in a chair in my consulting-room opposite a client. However, I have also gradually become aware that it is detrimental to *over*-analyse. This over-analysis of events occurs when the person goes over and over, again and again in her mind, the details of what has transpired. There is a technical term for that in cognitive behavioural therapy (CBT): rumination. This occurs when the individual develops an obsessive pattern of cognitions, and tends to repeatedly go over and over the same ground in her mind. It can often be discerned that a client has a proclivity towards this obsessive thinking especially during the hours of night. One of the reasons for this is that there are not so many things to distract a person while most of the population are sleeping, and it is usually impossible to take some remedial action during the night. It is not possible, for example, to make a phone-call to the GP to make an appointment and begin to take some action to alleviate anxious thoughts and fears.

Black and white thinking and catastrophising

There will be sections in Chapter Ten on these two "skewed" ways of thinking that may well have become "automatic" for some of our clients. This way of thinking also increases the fear of the fear cycle.

Patterns of behaviour that maintain and heighten stress

Taking avoidant action

The most common behavioural strategy that almost everyone who suffers from anxiety adopts is to take *avoidant action*. I mentioned earlier how, as a young woman in my early twenties, I became scared of the idea that I may vomit in a public place, in front of onlookers. The problem escalated and I developed full-blown agoraphobic symptoms because, without making a conscious decision, I instinctively adopted avoidant behaviour during the first two years of my illness. This effectively shut down my world in a progressive way, until the agoraphobia escalated to an extent where I found it extremely difficult to even take my dog for a short walk round the block. I had increasingly avoided scenarios that might lead to my feeling symptoms of anxiety, and thus my life "shut down". As this occurred, I became increasingly lacking in confidence about my coping mechanisms, and so in turn the vicious circle of avoidance grew ever larger and more encompassing. Fortunately, I then found the motivation to start to pull myself out of this repetitive cycle, by facing my fears instead of trying (but failing) to bury them and avoid them.

It is true that avoiding the stressful situation provides one with a short-term solution. But in the long-term, the difficulties are compounded and the stress becomes greater. It is understandable that the individual seeks to avoid, because this initially gives relief from the feelings of anxiety. However, in effect, such behaviour stores up greater problems in the long-term.

Use of alcohol or drugs

Many individuals start to rely on prescription drugs or over the counter (OTC) drugs to ease their stress and insomnia. This drug-taking sometimes even escalates—as I have seen several times in my life as a psychotherapist—to include the purchasing and use of illegal substances when the OTC drugs do not work any longer. Alternatively, this may occur when the GP stops prescribing the tranquillisers that your client has grown to rely upon. As I am sure you are aware, this is a slippery slope to escalating levels of difficulty, and as therapists, we need to be ever aware of any tendency in our clients to such behaviour and to counteract this.

Alcohol is, in effect, a legal drug that is imbibed in such quantities in today's society that individuals frequently do not appreciate that they are becoming dependent upon its effects. Again, in the short-term, it brings relief from stress and anxiety, as while under the influence of the substance, worries temporarily fade away. However, in the long-term alcohol is a depressant, plus the individual tends to need to consume ever larger amounts in order to maintain the same degree of relief from anxiety.

I am not saying, however, that there is never a place for the use of prescription drugs that a GP may offer. In the short-term, a tranquilliser may prove to be very effective. You should monitor your clients' use of these drugs with caution, and clearly state that they should not be over-used or used on a self-medication basis (i.e., I refer to the tendency for individuals to use increasing amounts of the tranquillisers in order to experience the relief of anxiety that they used to feel when taking the dose that the GP prescribed). However, if tranquillisers are used for a short time, to help while the individual is in a state of breakdown and before they can begin to use another mechanism to heal themselves, tranquilisers may provide what I term "a metaphoric walking stick to a person with a broken leg". Just as a walking stick will not heal a fracture, it will nevertheless help to ease one's progress through life temporarily while the leg is healing. Similarly a tranquilliser or anti-depressant may provide a temporary help in daily existence until the individual can tackle the problem using a more permanent solution. This may be in the form of CBT (such as the systematic desensitisation programme) or psychodynamic therapy.

CHAPTER FOUR

The labels: anxiety states and phobias

Panic attacks

When anxiety is experienced in a heightened form—when worry and repeated months or years of fear have taken their toll—the individual may suffer what is known as a panic attack.

Any of you, as therapists or clients, who have suffered such an experience, will not be able to forget how you felt during these periods of time. It may well be that you felt—as I did at first—that I was about to die. I felt that I would not, and could not, survive if I continued to feel like this. There is an inexplicable tendency to want to run away—though "where" precisely, one is not sure, except perhaps to the safety of home. The emphasis is upon escape from the awfulness that is being experienced in the moment. It is very difficult—or well-nigh impossible—to think clearly or reason things out during a panic attack. Thoughts race from one image to another; cognitive processes do not function. This mental confusion does not help the person to achieve their desperate wish to escape. In time, the sufferer may begin to have the awareness that this is what it means to experience "a panic attack".

Physiologically, there is a feeling of breathlessness; palms may be sweaty; nausea is common; as is dizziness and/or vertigo (spinning or a sense of being unbalanced; as if everything is moving slightly). There may be a fluttering sensation in the chest and a rapid heartbeat (palpitations); this may be accompanied by a tight feeling in the chest (and the individual often fears that she is suffering a heart attack and take herself to an accident and emergency department).

Added to all these physiological symptoms, there are likely to be accompanying psychological mechanisms at work that are confusing and difficult to bear. Perhaps the most unsettling is the psychological feeling of "derealisation": this involves a feeling of unreality, as if one is no longer in touch with or a part of the normal, everyday world. One can feel cut off from one's own sense of identity: this is known as "depersonalisation".

A lot of these feelings are caused by the rush of adrenaline; others come from the workings of the autonomic nervous system and what is known as the hypothalamic-pituitary-adrenal (HPA) axis. The HPA axis integrates the neurological and endocrine systems. The hypothalamus is a part of the brain that secretes hormones; these bind to the pituitary gland, which produces adrenocorticotrophic hormone (ACTH); in turn the adrenal glands produce cortisol. When enough cortisol has been produced, a negative feedback loop occurs in most people. The HPA axis produces less ACTH, and cortisol production is then lessened (O'Sullivan, 2015, pp. 196–197).

I will list below the feelings and sensations, which are all common when experiencing a panic attack:

- Sudden and intense feeling of fear.
- An overwhelming urge to "escape" and a wish to literally run away.
- The urge to be on the move; it seems awful to be stuck in one place.
- The person feels unsure about where she will feel safe even if she can escape.
- Tightness or sense of pressure in the chest.
- Palpitations (rapid heartbeat) or fluttering feeling in the chest. The individual can suffer tachycardia (uneven heartbeat).
- Feeling of breathlessness; as if one cannot get enough oxygen.
- Tunnel vision: the sufferer's peripheral vision has temporarily closed down.

- Light-headedness; the person often says to herself: "I feel really faint!"
- Racing thoughts and a feeling of confusion; "I can't think straight!"
- Irrational thoughts: as in "Am I going to die?", "Am I having a heart attack?", "Do I have cancer?", "Have I got some strange wasting disease which hasn't been diagnosed?"
- A sense of unreality; maybe a sense of impending doom. "I don't really seem a part of this world", "I don't understand what is happening!", "Something dreadful is about to happen!", "I don't feel like myself."
- Excessive sweating, perspiration.
- Muscle tension; feeling weak and shaky, as if one's legs will not support one any longer: trembling.
- Nausea. Occasionally, some individuals suffer actual vomiting.
- An urge to evacuate the bowels and/or bladder.

These feelings and thoughts, which delineate the nature of a panic attack, are some of the worst emotions that I have ever endured. However, I can tell you without doubt: they will not last forever. This is for the simple reason that all of these symptoms are as a result of an overdose of adrenaline, noradrenaline, and cortisol in your body (as described above and in Chapter Two). A panic attack is a manifestation of an extreme cycle of the "adrenaline cycle". The adrenal glands eventually grow tired and stop producing adrenaline. However, there is growing evidence that the HPA negative feedback loop does not perform adequately for some individuals, particularly those with psychosomatic symptoms (O'Sullivan, 2015).

In my case, repeated panic attacks soon developed into a phobia. However, just like so many others, I did not consciously appreciate this or give a name to what was happening to me for quite some time. After about a year of suffering these symptoms, I happened to find a book in the local library entitled *Self Help for your Nerves* by Claire Weekes (first published in 1962, and still available in an updated form). I remember being fascinated, as I read, in black-and-white, an accurate description of the way I was feeling. I experienced intense relief because of my realisation that I was not going mad, and that, furthermore, many others have known feelings like this as well. I write this book, in the hope that when some of you read it, you too will experience similar feelings of relief (if you are a sufferer) or alternatively, you will be able to help your client to appreciate the reasons that they are suffering this way and will be able to normalise the feelings. I have had the pleasure of giving a name of the nature of their suffering to many clients during my years in practice as a psychotherapist. Their relief is palpable.

Finding that book by Claire Weekes also helped me enormously to plan a way forward for myself. As a therapist, you can help your clients to the route to recovery. I sought the help of my GP, who had already prescribed tranquillisers but had not recommended any sort of therapy, or given me a diagnosis. With greater knowledge gained from reading this seminal text, I managed to secure a referral to a psychiatrist. The psychiatrist, in turn, compassionately referred me to a psychologist. It is to this lady, Anne (to whom I dedicate this book) that I owe my return to normal living. I remain eternally grateful for her help. She taught me the systematic desensitisation programme, which forms the central theme of this book.

After returning to work in the world of marketing, I spent a decade as a full-time mother. When I joined the ranks of the working world once again, I chose a completely different career from that which I had pursued as a younger person. I trained as a counsellor. This decision to change career was very much influenced by my own experience of psychological help at a crisis point in my life. My psychologist's help during my twenties has made such a difference to the way that I have been able to live my life, that I had become infused with a strong determination to help others, as I had been helped in my turn, to find a road back to psychic health.

My psychologist taught me the systematic desensitisation programme that I am going to describe in detail in Chapters Six and Seven. Then in Chapters Eight and Nine I present two case studies: both explain the journey back to normality of two of my clients: one suffering from agoraphobia, the other from a driving phobia. It will be no doubt be heartening to hear that during my twenty-seven years as a mental health professional I have been successful in helping many individuals to regain a pattern of normal living after they have consulted me in desperation, having lost all semblance of living an ordinary life that most people take for granted.

The reasons underlying the phobias and anxiety can be analysed as many and various. Each systematic desensitisation programme is devised specifically to cater for the specific nature of the anxiety and phobia from which each individual is suffering.

Helping clients who are suffering panic and severe anxiety only constitutes a part of my work as a psychotherapist. More generally in my practice, I concentrate upon working with individuals suffering from relationship difficulties, as I am a firm believer in Bowlby's attachment theory (Bowlby, 1979, 1988; Holmes, 1993). You can read about my approach to many clients' difficulties in *Attachment Theory: Working Towards Learned Security* (Fear, 2016). However, quite often, the two subjects—anxiety and relationship difficulties—run hand in hand. An individual who presents with concerns about her relationships and performance levels at work may actually be suffering from an underlying anxiety state or phobia. It may be this that is the unspoken cause of her difficulties, and it is quite regularly responsible for an unacceptable level of absenteeism from work, and the concurrent dissatisfaction of her employers. It is also not uncommon for one of the partners in a romantic couple to be suffering from an anxiety state, and we may well find that this is putting an intolerable strain upon their personal relationship.

While taking the manifestations of my phobic period into consideration, I cannot say that I am glad that I suffered such appalling panic attacks for five years during my young adult years, but I do feel satisfied by the fact that I have gained something positive from a situation that seemed totally negative at the time. It is, in fact, my philosophy for life (otherwise known as a world-view or a *weltanschauung*) to try to make something "good" out of something "bad" that happens in life. This way of perceiving the world was named by Frye (1957, 1964), who analysed Shakespearean literature, as an *ironic* world-view. Frye devised a typology that made it possible to divide one's type of worldview into four distinct outlooks. He gave the following names to the world views—*romantic, comic, tragic,* and *ironic* (Frye, 1957, 1964). Space does not permit me, in this book, to describe these differing world-views in detail. If you should be interested in finding out about them, then you can access some of the papers and chapters in edited books that I have published (Fear, 2015; Fear & Wolfe, 1996, 1999, 2000). Suffice it to say here that the individual who holds an ironic world-view examines what has taken place, and even though it may be unfortunate or even traumatic, he resolves to take something positive from the negative. It is a case of "turning the coin over, and looking at the other side" to see what you can gain positively from your experience.

This explains the rationale that I have adopted in order to make something "good" come from my "bad" experience of severe panic attacks in my twenties. As I have said, this has provided me with a strong motivation to write this book; I felt it is important to create the opportunity to share with a much bigger audience the way in which I found my way to recovery, so that many of you (both therapists and clients) can benefit too.

In the sections below in this chapter, I will outline for you the various common phobias from which different individuals suffer. I hope that these descriptions are helpful in enabling you to get to grips with the specific nature of your clients' problems, so that you can provide them with a label. So, as a first step, I suggest you give some serious thought to the specific nature of the fears that each individual is suffering. What is actually happening, or what do they fear may happen, that leads their pituitary and adrenal glands together to release an overload of adrenaline and noradrenaline? The stress that they suffer in consequence releases a third harmful hormone: cortisol (through the action of the HPA axis).

You may experience a struggle to find the trigger or "gain" underlying the client's conscious rationalisation of why she has stopped going to work. As their therapist, it is your role to help her to face up to the nature of her conflict. It may well be that your client suffers a barely conscious trigger associated with a past event, or she may derive some gain from defining herself as an "ill person". She may well be displacing the reasons for changed behaviour on to more rational, understandable, and "believable" fears such as being afraid of a bullying boss; of feeling that they cannot cope with a new role at work; that in recent times they have fallen out with work colleagues. Understandably, this gives the impression that what is happening in her external world is not the result of anything within her locus of control. It is far easier to say this than to admit (for example) that she is afraid of going to work because she may suffer a fainting attack. Here is an example of the use of the defence mechanism of displacement that I have frequently seen at work in my psychotherapy practice; the person moves from the reality of what is happening and replaces it with something that seems more socially acceptable.

I will now move on to a description of a number of phobias and heightened anxiety states. The list I employ is not exhaustive, and you (as a client or a therapist) may well describe a phobia that has not been awarded a distinctive name, and that is not found in a book on anxiety and phobia. Alternatively, an individual may suffer from a combination of phobias—for example, there may be a fear of going to the supermarket (for fear of being caught up in a queue at the checkout) combined with a fear of visiting the cinema or theatre. In fact, such combinations can usually be analysed so that you come to appreciate that the underlying fear amounts to one and the same dread: perhaps a fear of fainting or feeling foolish in a confined environment, and of not being able to escape without attracting attention.

Agoraphobia

This word is a translation from the Greek words, *agora* and *phobia*, and literally means *fear of the market place*. This does not indicate, however, that one only fears entering and staying within a market-place or, to use the modern idiom, a shopping centre.

Agoraphobia is commonly understood as a fear of open spaces. However, in fact this is rarely true. Most individuals who suffer from agoraphobia fear going to any place other than the space that they have personally designated as "safe". Commonly, the individual believes that the only safe place is "home". The result of this is that the individual finds increasingly that she tends to stay at home and starts, gradually, to fear going out anywhere, regardless of the destination. This fear usually spreads over time, so that there grows to be an increasing number of places that are deemed unsafe. The individual may begin by feeling fearful at the idea of fainting, or vomiting, or defecating, or losing control in some other way. Then the person may reason to themselves, "I will not travel by bus to work in case I faint". Then the fear starts to encompass travelling by car, and then develops into a fear of going out for a walk. This state of affairs is reached because often the first reaction to fear is to *avoid* the situation that causes anxiety. However, when the individual takes avoidant action, the fears start to multiply, and a vicious circle spirals out of control, with the individual becoming increasingly fearful and avoidant. An effect of adopting an avoidant strategy is that there is no opportunity to face the fear and learn that it is possible to surmount it. This latter course of action would facilitate, in fact, the development of coping skills. With practice, one finds that the anxious feelings disappear, to be replaced by feelings of confidence.

In fact, what I have described above about taking an *avoidant strategy* to try to deal with agoraphobia, applies to each and every phobia or situation that causes extreme anxiety. As I will show you in Chapters Six and Seven, it is only by helping your clients to face their fears, and find a way of tackling them, that you can help them to grasp the capacity to recover and end a situation where their lives are dominated by fear.

Agoraphobia may develop as a result of any sort of traumatic situation. One person may have seen someone taken ill with a stroke, heart attack, or an epileptic fit. They may have been present when someone was vomiting or fainting. The fear then escalates to the notion that this may happen to them. Indeed, agoraphobia may alternatively arise because your client has been taken ill while in a shopping centre, or are at the theatre. They may have felt ashamed at the loss of control, or have felt deeply embarrassed at the need to escape from the middle of a row at the cinema. A phobia may develop as a result of the individual suffering a first panic attack in a public place. As time goes by, she may find herself going to great lengths to try to avoid the feelings of unreality from overcoming her again.

Equally, the underlying cause of the development of a phobia may lie in some related trauma in childhood. Alternatively, it may arise as a result of the daily impact of a separate health problem that affects an individual's life (e.g., multiple sclerosis). An event in childhood, such as an incident of abuse, or a family feud, may lay hidden for many years yet be the underlying cause of a phobia. This is known as a trigger. Defence mechanisms such as denial, displacement, repression, and sublimation may be at play. It then requires some detailed psychodynamic work to enable the client to remember the event within the trusting, safe and contained environment of the consulting room. As a therapist, you will be able to help your client (via a process of free association) to pinpoint the underlying significance of past events. However, while psychodynamic work is helpful in enabling your client to get a sense of the root cause of her phobia, it is not necessary in order to put a systematic desensitisation programme into action. I did not analyse the root causes of my phobia until many years after my recovery using a systematic desensitisation programme. However, finding the root cause *did* give me a huge sense of satisfaction as the "completion of the jigsaw puzzle".

If we analyse the feelings that an agoraphobic person suffers, beneath it all, is the fear of losing control. This fear of loss of control is, in fact, at the root of many panic attacks from which a phobia develops. As a therapist, you need to teach the concept that the fear that "it" will happen again is often remote in actuality. In fact, it is very likely that no such thing will happen again for a long time, if ever. We need as therapists to help our clients to *regain a sense of proportion*, and to learn to "reality-test" their fears. I can provide a case study of this by telling you of the way I helped a young woman who presented in counselling when she been unable to go to work for nine months. We discovered after some sessions that the root of this fear was the result of a single incident of severe and embarrassing diarrhoea while at work, and she had become afraid that this would recur. This was compounded by other stresses in her life, including stress in her relationship with her partner. Gradually, she was able to trust enough to be able to recognise and name the trigger of her anxiety, and by talking through the issue and finding solutions to her stresses, plus by the application of a systematic desensitisation programme, we worked together to find a way to solve her difficulties. She was able to return to work and normal living.

Claustrophobia

Claustrophobia, in some ways, is commonly thought to be at the opposite end of the spectrum from agoraphobia. This would be so if agoraphobia were really the fear of open spaces. Claustrophobia is a fear of enclosed spaces. However, agoraphobia is more accurately described as a fear of *public places*. In consequence, the two phobias often overlap. People often speak of the fear of being in a severely enclosed space such as a lift. However, this enclosed space may also be constituted by a "room" such as a cinema, a theatre auditorium, or a restaurant. Once again, as in agoraphobia, the fear is of not being able to escape, particularly of not being able to achieve a getaway without drawing attention to oneself. Once again, we are talking about the fear of loss of control.

Emetophobia (fear of vomit and vomiting) and fainting phobia

The above phobias are a lot more common than you may appreciate in your work with clients. Again, the root cause, if one analyses it, is the fear of loss of control. Many of us (including ourselves as therapists) also tend to fear embarrassment, or that other people will "think me stupid". Many individuals who are suffering from phobia have made this comment to me, feeling (unnecessarily but understandably) foolish as they utter these very words.

In fact, if you faint while out in public, or at work, or on the train, then the vast majority of people will come to your aid, and help you out. In fact, humanity is generally enormously understanding, and helpful, when one of us suffers something really unpleasant.

Fifteen years ago, I fell down a grating in Worcester while out on a shopping trip. I smashed my four front teeth and cut my nose and upper lip badly. Three separate individuals ran to my aid, comforting me and calling an ambulance. They stayed with me until further help was at hand. They could not have been kinder. I admit—I felt embarrassed—but I did not suffer any after-effects of phobia, probably because I had endured my years of phobia when I was in my twenties, and had learned from the systematic desensitisation programme that one is far better advised to face the fear, and enlist some support. And above all, I have learned that the majority of the population are well-meaning.

Social anxiety phobia

There is often an overlap between those who suffer from agoraphobia and social anxiety phobia. The latter usually begins as a result of feeling it is very difficult to speak out; or finding making conversation with unfamiliar individuals really embarrassing. It may result as a consequence of a specific incident when the individual felt particularly isolated at a social event, such as a wedding reception or party.

Many of us do not look forward to social functions, and tend to avoid them if possible. However, there is a difference between the person who will avoid a social gathering if they "just do not feel like it this weekend", and someone who shies away from any social function, whatever it may be, even if it involves close friends or relatives. It is all a question of degree. Many of us do not relish attending a party that others cannot wait for. It depends whether one avoids it at all costs, or whether one decides sometimes to attend such functions, such as on occasions when under an obligation to family or business.

Social phobia is sometimes associated with a personal fear of blushing or shaking (tremor). There is also a tendency for the individual to feel that they "know" that others think they are a fool; silly; stupid. As a therapist, you may be able to help your client to analyse that maybe she catches herself "mind-reading" or "fortune-telling". Through the therapeutic relationship, you need to convince your client that no-one can read minds. Similarly, no-one can tell fortunes—and accurately predict what is going to happen next.

It is common for social phobia to be associated with a time in life when the person is suffering a loss of self-esteem or self-confidence, either temporarily or permanently. You need, in consequence, to help your client to tackle the reasons underlying low self-esteem. They might like to try an assertiveness course. I persuaded one of my clients recently to attend a week-end course on assertiveness, and from that we went on to help her learn mechanisms by which she could stand up for herself in the workplace. I will present more ideas about this in Chapter Ten on cognitive interventions.

Social phobia can also result from feelings of fear or inadequacy about giving a talk to a roomful of people, or from being asked to present at a seminar. Fear of public speaking is actually very common—and it is also difficult for many people to comfortably air their opinions within a group. However, not everyone who feels like this is actually suffering from social phobia. Phobia lies at one end of the continuum; at the other end lies the individual who just prefers not to speak in public.

Supermarket phobia and shopping centre phobia

Your client may be finding that she is scared of going to the supermarket for the weekly shop for groceries. I need to make it clear again that any of these phobias and anxiety states can also happen to males. In fact, a client whom I worked with who suffered a pronounced supermarket phobia was indeed male. He tried at first to cope with the phobia by ordering his supplies online. However, as so often occurs, the phobia then spread to other areas, and so it needed to be tackled.

Similarly, your client may find that she has developed a phobia about shopping centres, particularly the huge enclosed ones such as

Westfield in London, or Lakeside in Essex. This phobia may gradually, over a period of time, extend to cover all shopping venues.

Again, this phobia is usually a function of an individual being scared of losing control in a place where, to some extent, they feel exposed and under scrutiny. One of my clients ("Yvonne") was unfortunate enough to be sexually assaulted while she was abroad on holiday, in a strange environment, and far from the safety of home. For a number of reasons, she was unable to institute any legal proceedings, which left her with feelings of inadequacy and inability to protect herself. By the time she arrived at my consulting room, she was starting to avoid visiting any public places, including the town in which she had lived all her life. At first she did not connect the social phobia to the incident of sexual assault but we were soon able to make links to the root cause of her fears. She also engaged in a systematic desensitisation programme, which enabled her to resume normal life within a short space of time. This included her ability to return to work, which she had been unable to do for several months, feeling too anxious to put herself into the public arena of the workplace.

Hypochondriasis

Hypochondriasis is the formal name given to a person suffering from an irrational and pronounced fear that she has, or will shortly suffer from, some dread disease. It is characterised by an excessive anxiety about one's state of health. In my experience as a therapist, it commonly occurs after an individual has born witness to a close friend or relative who dies a prolonged, painful death. Others of us may suffer from hypochondriasis as a result of having an unusually acute awareness of our bodily functions. This is often combined with a cognitive tendency towards catastrophising (mentally "jumping ahead" to fear that the worst scenario one can imagine will actually come true).

While it is good policy for all of us to be health aware, and for women (for example) to regularly check their breasts for signs of change, and to attend appointments for breast screening, one enters another realm when one is consistently and repeatedly dreading that one is actually suffering yet another new illness. In this case, the fear of illness has taken on an obsessive quality.

Obsessional compulsive disorder (OCD)

While this is not known technically as a phobia, I am including it in my descriptions of various heightened anxiety states.

Individuals who suffer OCD tend to feel compelled to carry out particular rituals in order to feel able, say, to leave home without a sense of overwhelming anxiety. This may present as self-imposed rituals (such as checking the locks on the doors and windows, or re-checking that all the electrical sockets are switched off before leaving the home). Maybe one's OCD is composed of carrying out a series of tasks in a certain, prescribed order (a ritual), or having the need to conjure up a series of metal images (known as ruminations). The individual needs first of all to come to accept that she is suffering from OCD. Until your client accepts that she has a problem, she cannot hope to find a solution to it, and she will be reluctant to enter into any programme.

Common OCD symptoms feature a need to repeatedly wash one's body or clothes, particularly after having defecated. The individual may develop complicated and very time-consuming rituals, which they feel compelled to work through, before they can emerge into the everyday world without excruciating anxiety.

Another common OCD symptom evolves gradually because of an unrealistic fear about being contaminated by bacteria. The pattern of OCD is often identifiable by the individual compulsively washing their hands many times each day. The skin on the hands then becomes red, sore, and cracks from this compulsion to repeatedly wash them. GP's can often start to diagnose the OCD by noticing this physical manifestation during a consultation on an entirely different subject. I have also worked with individuals who have insisted that their family members remove all their clothes when they come into the home, in the fear that the outside world may contaminate their home.

OCD can take many forms, and space does not permit me to mention all its ramifications. However, it is true to say that OCD has a life-shattering effect upon many of the population. OCD, and all the phobias, are more readily tackled if the client presents for therapy soon after the unhelpful way of life takes over. The longer an individual has suffered, the longer it is likely that it will take to beat the "bad" (unproductive, dysfunctional) habit and replace it with a "good" habit.

Generalised anxiety disorder (GAD)

If your client is suffering from GAD, it is likely that they describe themselves as "a natural worrier". It is a syndrome used to describe those of us when we find ourselves suffering persistent feelings of anxiety, worry, and "What if . . .?" thoughts about diverse subjects and situations in our lives.

It is natural for all of us to worry about some aspects of our lives (such as our careers, partnerships, health, families)—it is just that when one is suffering from GAD, worries are triggered constantly, and are the result of irrational thought processes. Again, it is a question of degree.

The first help that you can offer your client is to analyse with her co-operation what sort of situations trigger her anxieties. Sometimes, individuals believe it is dangerous to focus on their worries, but I am positive that it will actually do no harm and it is the first step towards recovery. There is often a sort of "magical thinking" that the "thing" will not happen if they do not consciously acknowledge it. This is a superstition that has no grounding in reality, but it helps if you can enable the client to admit to such beliefs without feeling too foolish.

It is useful for us as therapists to *analyse* the nature of the "worry", so that we can accurately assess, with the client, the chance of "it" actually occurring. You are teaching the skills of reality-testing. Some use of *distraction techniques* can also be useful—transferring the thoughts on to something else. *Mindfulness meditation* can also provide a way of minimising anxiety. As a therapist, you can also help your client to put into practice the relaxation exercises in Chapter Six. This is a fail-safe method of reducing anxiety and a crucial role you can play is that of motivating your client to maintain her level of commitment to learn the skills of progressive relaxation. It can be helpful if you first, as a therapist, familiarise yourself with the exercises.

Post-traumatic stress disorder (PTSD)

Once again, PTSD is not a phobia, but it is an anxiety disorder, that affects many individuals at some time in life. It shares some symptoms with panic.

Post-traumatic stress disorder was first identified in war veterans. Those soldiers and airmen who fought in the First World War returned from the battlefields with what was then referred to as "shell-shock". During and after the Second World War, Wilfred Bion and colleagues helped soldiers in a pioneering way to recover from the symptoms of mental illness that they were suffering after the traumas of war at a specialised unit in Selly Oak, Birmingham. The ideas about treating PTSD have developed from those beginnings.

While some servicemen and women still nowadays suffer from PTSD as a result of traumas witnessed and experienced first-hand in wars such as Afghanistan or Iraq, this illness now covers others that are ill as a result of traumas in which they have been involved or have witnessed. The same symptoms, characterised particularly by frequent flash-backs and nightmares, are experienced whatever the cause of PTSD, along with other symptoms common to all phobias. The symptoms include finding it hard to concentrate; to recall details of life readily; psychosomatic induced pain; sweating; trembling and rapid heartbeat. PTSD affects a third of individuals who suffer a car accident, sexual assault, mugging, sexual abuse, or participate as an onlooker or victim of events such as "7/7" in London, or any other terrorist incident or natural disaster (e.g., tornados or floods).

Symptoms of PTSD can occur directly after the precipitating event, but can also begin some months or even years later. I have worked with SAS officers who served their country for years and seemed unaffected; then suddenly they start to be struck down by the symptoms of PTSD. It requires the help of a psychotherapist or counsellor to work in a psychodynamic format through the underlying issues that have caused this apparent breakdown in normal functioning, in order to enable the individual to recover permanently. However, a systematic desensitisation programme can also help enormously to counteract the phobic symptoms that such clients frequently encounter as well.

A list of other phobias

The list below consists of the names of phobias to specific objects or situations:

- Apiphobia—fear of bees.
- Arachnophobia—fear of spiders.
- Brontophobia—fear of thunder.
- Haematophobia—fear of blood (as portrayed by Martin Clunes in the *Doc Martin* television series).
- Hydrophobia—fear of water.
- Ophidophobia—fear of snakes.
- Ornithophobia—fear of birds.

The problem with some of the above-mentioned phobias is that if one treats them via a systematic desensitisation programme, one cannot plan in advance for the client to carry out the task because one does not know when the feared object will appear. For example, it is impossible for any of us to predict with accuracy when we are going to suffer thundery weather. It is still possible to use a systematic desensitisation programme, but it may need to be modified to a process known as "exposure therapy" or "flooding". It is therefore sometimes helpful to use photographic images of the feared situation or creature, or realistic models, for example, of a snake or a spider. It is also possible to arrange trips to pet shops so that the client can be in close contact with the feared object.

Similarly, in the case of flying phobia, it is often possible to help the client arrange to take part in a specific course dealing with this that has been organised by an airline. This usually involves a weekend where fears of flying are discussed; participants are introduced to a mock-up of an airline interior, and are finally encouraged to take part in an actual short flight in an aeroplane, accompanied by staff trained to reassure and answer concerns.

CHAPTER FIVE

Involving the general practitioner: the helpfulness and limitations of medications

Introduction

While this book deals largely with the ways in which you can help your clients deal with their problems with anxiety, there are also times in which you are well advised to recommend that they consult their GP or other health professional, such as Community Psychiatric Nurse (CPN), or Psychological Well-being Practitioner.

Consulting the GP

It is a wise option for you to enlist the help of your client's GP for a number of reasons, and to encourage your client to make a friend of him or her. Ethically, from your own point of view as a counsellor or psychotherapist, it is wise to ask all of your clients for permission to make a note of their GP and his/her practice so that you have someone to contact and advise you if your client should ever suffer from suicidal ideation. In this way, should this become a reality, you have someone with whom to share some responsibility for the welfare of your client and any steps she may take to end her life. I recommend that you explain the limits of confidentiality to your client at their initial assessment appointment with you. I make it clear that in the event of my believing that my client may harm themselves or someone else, I may deem it appropriate to break the confidentiality contract, although I will do my best to speak to them first (you also need to talk through your use of a supervisor, explaining that no names, occupations, or other distinguishing features are discussed). I am sure that many of you now provide your clients with a contract at their first appointment that lays down these very necessary guidelines and makes the limits of confidentiality and commitments regarding payment and cancellation periods clear to them. If the contract is only verbal, it is very easily forgotten or misinterpreted perhaps as a result of the distress that the client is probably feeling at the outset of counselling. It also may prove useful insurance if you should unfortunately become the subject of a complaint.

Regarding your client consulting their GP, it needs to be explained that their GP can only help them if they are honest in expressing their concerns. It is all too common for patients to launch into a description of some other nefarious physical symptom out of sheer embarrassment. You need to remind them that a GP's time is limited usually to a ten minute appointment, so it is wise to recommend that they make a list of the points that they would like to cover. It is not embarrassing or unusual for GP's to be aware that their patients present with a list, and refer to it during the consultation. If your client feels the need, she may be able to request a double-length interview with the doctor at the time of booking the appointment.

You need to reassure your client that a good GP will not dismiss symptoms as trifling, or of no consequence, but give his genuine attention to the ways in which he can offer help. It is quite usual that at first he may order blood tests, urine tests, or other diagnostic tools in order to be able to diagnose whether symptoms have a physiological cause. Similar symptoms can be evidenced, for example, when one is suffering from hyperthyroidism (overactive thyroid function) or hypothyroidism (underactive thyroid function), or diabetes. GPs have trained for many years so that they are able to ask the correct questions and carry out the appropriate medical tests, before they will conclude that symptoms have a psychological basis. However, statistics evidence that up to 50% of patients' consultations are with reference to problems that have a psychological or psychosomatic cause. This should not mean that psychological symptoms are taken any less seriously because they do not have an organic cause.

Once the GP has diagnosed that your client is suffering from psychological difficulties, he may well be able to offer you some help in the form of medication, or access to talking therapies. Unfortunately, because of lack of resources in the NHS at present, access to GP counselling and NHS psychological help is severely limited. However, you can encourage your client to consult her physician about the use of counselling and psychotherapy. In Chapter Eleven I talk about finding professional help through private channels for any reader of this book who is actually suffering from panic or phobia themselves.

Types of medication

Medications for psychological difficulties are listed below under a number of subject headings. I give examples of the names of the types of drugs that your client's doctor may feel it is appropriate to prescribe, and what these various drug groups aim to achieve.

Beta-blockers

Beta-blockers were originally prescribed to relieve high blood pressure. They are also used for migraine prophylaxis. However, nowadays they are also prescribed by the medical profession to combat the physical symptoms of anxiety, such as profuse sweating, trembling, and palpitations. They may cause the side-effect of feelings of lethargy for the first couple of weeks, and individuals sometimes suffer weakness in the limbs. This is because they slow down the pulse rate and reduce blood pressure. While they are helpful in lessening the physical symptoms that accompany anxiety, they will not alter your client's thought processes, so they do not cure—just make life more tolerable while the underlying problems are tackled.

Examples of names of drugs in this category are propranolol and atenolol.

Tranquillisers

Sedatives such as diazepam (Valium) act on receptors in the brain called neurotransmitters, which in turn relax the muscles and produce a feeling of calm. They mostly belong to a class of drugs known as benzodiazepines. They are very effective in the short-term, but the GP's hesitation in prescribing this category of drug lies in the fact that they are highly addictive, and some individuals tend to need ever-increasing doses in order to continue to experience the same calming effect.

In the 1970s and 1980s, tranquillisers were frequently prescribed, so that, as the Rolling Stones intoned, they were viewed "as mothers' little helper". However, since the addictive nature of these drugs has been recognised, physicians tend to only be prepared to prescribe them on a short-term basis to help an individual over the immediate period of trauma. They should not be taken for over four months.

Anti-depressants

There are two main types of anti-depressant that are prescribed for anxiety. While these drugs are primarily prescribed for depression, now that tranquillisers are no longer freely available, the anxiety-reducing concomitant effect of these drugs means that they are commonly prescribed to help patients with anxiety.

Tricyclic antidepressants

Pills such as amitriptyline or dosulepin are prescribed, particularly if the individual is having difficulty in getting to sleep or staying asleep. They tend to make most individuals feel very sleepy at first (even in the day-time), but in the longer term, they help patients to sleep more deeply and relax their muscles.

Selective serotonin reuptake inhibitors (SSRI's) and selective noradrenaline inhibitors (SNRI's)

This class of anti-depressant also helps to lessen anxiety. Certain chemicals in the brain act both as hormones and neurotransmitters, and two of these—serotonin and noradrenaline—can improve mood and emotional well-being. These drugs increase the level of serotonin in the brain. Serotonin is known as "the feel-good chemical", and one theory exists that depression is caused by low levels of serotonin.

Both types of these drugs take several weeks to work, so your client can expect to feel no better for at least three weeks. However, many individuals have regarded them as wonder drugs, and when the best known: Prozac (fluoxetine) was first released on to the market, it was considered by many to be a wonder-drug.

Both sorts of drugs—the SSRIs and the SNRIs—can make the individual suffer from numerous side-effects. It is a matter for the individual to decide which causes the greater misery: the side effects or the anxiety. They do, indeed, help many individuals to cope with their anxiety.

The choices among alternative therapies

The drugs mentioned above can only be accessed via a GP or other physician or psychiatrist. The tablets that I mention below are, at the moment, available without a doctor's prescription, over the counter (OTC).

If one looks in the shelves of the chemist's shops in the sections that stock vitamin supplements, it is possible to find a range of drugs that one can try. One of drugs which has been on the shelves for many years now is the compound known by its trade name of Kalms. Most of these supplements combine a variety of herbal preparations such as valerian, passiflora, hops, and St. John's Wort. Research shows that St. John's Wort is as effective for mild to moderate depression as the SSRI's. However, I offer a word of warning. It is dangerous to take this supplement in combination with a number of prescription drugs; included in this list is any other prescribed anti-depressant. It can increase the level of serotonin to a dangerous level, so that one can suffer serotonin syndrome, which in some rare cases can prove fatal. Also, St. John's Wart renders the birth control pill ineffective.

There are supplements on the market that consists of Rhodiola Root. It is available under the brand name of Vitano, or from health food shops such as Holland and Barrett as Rhodiola Rosea. Some of my patients have found this very effective to use in times of mild anxiety.

Some individuals believe that a preparation known as 5HTP works very well. I cannot comment on this as I have no knowledge of it myself, only anecdotal evidence. Again, other individuals find that the ashwagandha herb proves very useful in reducing their anxiety.

There are also several supplements available to help lessen the effects of sleepless nights. As I have said before, they include a variety of herbs such as passiflora, gentian, valerian, and hops. Again, I have heard positive comments about a herbal preparation called Restful Sleep. However, it is wise to note that one should not use these preparations other than in the short-term.

CHAPTER SIX

Breathing and relaxation

Deep breathing

Many people, when very anxious, involuntarily start to hyperventilate. It is partially as a result of this that an individual feels breathless during a panic attack as if she cannot catch her breath. In reality the individual is suffering from too high a concentration of oxygen in relation to the carbon dioxide in her system. In order to stop this, you can help as a therapist by teaching your client to breathe into a paper bag (not a plastic bag, because this can be dangerous and lead to suffocation). When one breathes into a paper bag for a few minutes, rather than into the atmosphere, it changes the ratio of carbon dioxide to oxygen in the blood. One breathes back the carbon dioxide that is in the bag.

It can also help to tell your client to practise what is known as seven to eleven breathing. This entails inhaling to the count of seven, and then exhaling, counting from seven to eleven. Your client will become calmer if she does this for a few minutes. It can also be carried out less visibly than making use of a paper bag. As a consequence of breathing in this way, your client will start to feel less panicky.

However, in the longer term, it is wise to teach your client the art of "belly breathing" (abdominal breathing) or "controlled breathing". This entails breathing more deeply, so that the person makes sure that she feels the distention of her abdomen as she breathes. You can instruct your client to place a hand on the abdomen she that she can actually feel her abdomen inflating and deflating.

It is essential that you recommend that your client practises this breathing for a couple of weeks, for five minutes several times a day, so that she gets used to the rhythm and sense of breathing more deeply. Naturally, because it will be a new sensation, it may feel strange at first. You can assure your client that there is nothing to be alarmed about: this is quite normal, but because of her heightened sensitivity to change; any change in bodily sensation may seem strange at first and tend to make her feel anxious. I cannot stress enough; this needs to be practised. As I have said earlier in the book: practice, practice, practice are the necessary watchwords.

I appreciate that your client may feel that this advice sounds very boring, and may feel that such a simple measure as breathing correctly will not help to alleviate her symptoms. In fact, learning to belly-breath will help on numerous occasions to calm the mind and body— the two elements of all of us that are so often entwined.

You can advise your client to follow the short typical list of recommendations below. It might help to provide her with a short list of instructions so that she can refer to these at home.

Suggested list of instructions

- Make sure that you use your lungs fully, and avoid the tendency to breathe from the upper chest alone.
- Concentrate on breathing smoothly, without any gulps or gasps.
- At first, it is most efficacious to do this exercise in either a lying down or sitting position. I suggest that you choose from these two positions whichever feels "most normal". Once used to practising, you will find that you can carry out the exercise while standing, and additionally, you can use it while out in the street as you are shopping, walking, and just feeling overcome with anxiety.
- Place one hand on your chest and the other on your belly. This will enable you to carry out the exercise most effectively and

accurately, because you will be able to feel the rise and fall of your abdomen as you breathe.

- Breathe in slowly, but fully, through your nose. Feel your abdomen inflate, and take pleasure in this breathing. You can even carry out an associated mantra as you do this, such as: "I feel calm. I feel relaxed. I am going to be all right".
- Breathe out through your nose too—ensuring that your breathing is slow and even.
- If it suits you, when you are practising deep breathing (as opposed to ordinary breathing), it can be helpful to count to seven with your inhalation, and then to go on counting up from seven to eleven as you exhale.
- Repeat this practice for several minutes, several times per day, as it can prove to be very calming. Remember to begin breathing to the seven to eleven pattern when you are feeling panicky. It really helps to slow down the feelings of panic.
- When you are concentrating upon your ordinary breathing, in order to be sure that you have the right combination of oxygen and carbon dioxide in your body, it is wise to aim for ten to twelve breaths per minute. If it helps, you can slowly count up to three on the in-breath, and three again on the out-breath. Make sure that you are not breathing too rapidly because this may make you feel faint. You need to do this several times a day, for several weeks, so that you learn the rhythm of breathing in this way.

You need to stress to your client that she needs to practise this breathing several times a day, for several weeks. She will then give her body a chance to lose a "bad" habit and begin to feel that a new, "good" habit is normal. This takes time. It may sound simple to your client, but as you are aware, it requires real effort to change a habit.

It may help your client if you arrange for her to have some sort of aide-memoire so that she remembers to carry out this exercise several times a day. You can suggest that she programmes in a reminder on her mobile phone or wears her wrist watch on the other arm for a while, so that each time she glances at her wrist-watch, its changed position will remind her to take a few moments to practise the exercise again. Other people have found that putting a spot of nail varnish on the face of their watch performs the trick of an aide-memoire.

Learning the art of relaxation

It is an essential forerunner of the systematic desensitisation programme that you first of all teach your client to be able to relax at will—so that she can become able to identify when muscles are tense. It will then be within her conscious control to relax her muscles at will. This very exercise will give her a sense of control over her body that she is doubtless not enjoying at the moment.

It is very likely—most likely, in fact—that at the moment your client describes herself as feeling tense most of the time, but she may not even recognise the tension until she is suffering a full-blown panic attack. Many of us at generally do not recognise tension when we feel it—this is because we have not labelled it as such, and are not familiar with analysing our feelings (especially our bodily feelings).

It is essential that you stress to your client that she practises, practises, practises! I know that what I am asking you to teach sounds repetitive and may sound tedious. However, having learned the skill of deep relaxation when I was twenty-three, I have in fact found it an invaluable skill many, many times ever since.

Teach the following guidelines regarding relaxation:

- First of all, decide on a place within your home where you are comfortable and you can be quiet and uninterrupted. At first, it may most helpful to carry out this exercise lying down on a bed, because then if you have a few spare minutes after the exercise, you may enjoy a short nap.

- You need to carry out this exercise *at least twice a day for several weeks*. It generally takes four weeks to feel that you can command your body.

- Choose somewhere that is quiet, and not too warm or too chilly. If you are cold, it is very hard to relax.

- Take off your shoes, and indeed, you may find it helpful to remove any clothes that feel constrictive.

- Avoid practising these relaxation exercises just after a meal, or when you feel tired and hassled because, for example, you have just put the children to bed, and you probably feel pressurised to finish off some other tasks.

- Breathe in the way I have taught earlier. Remember to inflate your abdomen, and to breathe slowly (not shallowly) through your nose, both on the in-breath and the out-breath.

- Try to adopt a "passive" state of mind: for the ten minutes of this exercise, forget your mental "To Do" list. Just concentrate on the exercise.

You may like to tell your client that this method of relaxation was first devised by a man called Edmund Jacobsen in the 1930s. Your client can appreciate that this is a very old, tried and tested method that is used by most psychologists and CBT counsellors to help clients to gain the advantages of relaxation. You might like to learn the following way of teaching this programme, so that you can help your client by carrying it out the first time with them in your consulting room. It may even help to repeat this with your client for a few sessions, if you feel that they are reluctant to practise at home.

Below is a transcript of what you might say. Of course, you will adjust your wording to suit your own way of speaking:

Once lying down (or sitting, if you find that feels more normal), pay attention to your muscles. This method of relaxation is commonly referred to as "the tense then let-go" method of relaxation of each muscle group. We are going to work through your muscle groups, starting at your feet and working up to your head, by focusing on one muscle group at a time. You first tense that group of muscles, and then consciously try to relax them.

Start with your *feet: curl up your toes* for fifteen seconds, feeling the tension in your muscles, and then let go, consciously trying to relax them. Notice the difference between the feeling of tension—the "tight" feeling—and the relaxed feeling.

Next, stretch your feet out, as if *pointing your toes* away from your body. Tense, then relax (fifteen seconds tense; fifteen seconds relax).

Then move on to your *lower legs*. Tense the *calf muscles and your knees*, and then let go.

Next, think about your *thigh muscles*. Carry out the same exercise of tense and relax. Take the time to appreciate the difference between the feelings of tension and the feelings of relaxation.

Then your *abdomen*: tense your *stomach muscles* by pulling them up, trying to make your abdomen hard. Then let those muscles go limp.

Your back: arch your back, bringing back your shoulders and feeling the sense of stretch in your muscles. Then relax.

Shoulders and neck: shrug your shoulders, and if you were indicating to someone that you cannot be bothered! Then *press your head back,* thus tensing the muscles in your neck. Tense, then let go.

Arms: stretch your arms out, both together. Feel the tension in your fingers and hands by stretching them out, *splaying your fingers.* Tense for fifteen seconds, then let go for fifteen seconds. Feel the difference in the sensation.

Face: tense up your facial muscles by *grinning* like the Cheshire Cat in *Alice in Wonderland* (don't worry, no-one will see you do this!). *Raise your eyebrows,* as if in surprise at something startling that someone has said. Tense, then let go.

At the end of this routine, allow yourself a few minutes to get used to the greater feeling of relaxation that your body now is enjoying. You may gradually feel that the exercise infuses you with a sense of warmth. In any case, you will start to recognise, after a few days, the difference between tense muscles and relaxed ones.

You will find that this exercise brings untold benefits. You need to learn this exercise as a very necessary forerunner to embarking on the full systematic desensitisation programme. However, over the coming years you will realise that it is invaluable in helping you to get to sleep in times of stress; before job interviews; before public speaking.

If you still feel tense at the end of the routine, simply repeat the whole exercise by doing it again. Persevere, because you may well not start to experience a sense of deep relaxation until you have been doing these exercises for five to seven days. Remember, this is not a competition; you will not get into trouble if you find it hard at first. You will not feel the major benefits of this until you have practised for at least two weeks.

A shorter version of this exercise

When your client has practised this exercise for two to four weeks, at least twice a day, she will find that she is now able to recognise the difference between muscles that are tense (tight) from those that are relaxed. Explain that she will then be able to begin to be capable of relaxing at will.

When I first started to carry out this exercise, it would take me at least ten minutes of going through the muscle groups systematically before I could feel any real sense of difference. After a month of assiduous practice, I could reduce the tension in my body within a minute of just sitting, calmly, but being aware of my body, and "letting go".

A note on bio-feedback machines and relaxation CDs

It is possible, if your client's financial circumstances allow, for her to purchase a bio-feedback machine from the internet. This is a device that you strap to your finger (or arm) using Velcro. It works on the basis that one's skin resistance differs when one is tense, from when one is relaxed (i.e., the machine registers skin resistance). When you are tense, it emits a shrill, constant noise, which gradually changes to a lower single tone and then silence, as you become more relaxed. You learn to focus on reducing the noise from a shrill constant tone to silence as quickly as possible. It is a behavioural tool, just like the Russian scientist, Pavlov, famously invented to teach his dog when food was available.

It is a good device for helping the individual to speedily learn to recognise when they are tense, as opposed to when they are relaxed. This will enable your client to learn how to control muscle tension quite quickly. While it is a useful aid, that I have tested and used myself, do not think that it is a necessary adjunct to being able to learn to relax.

Alternatively, for just a few pounds, your client can buy a relaxation CD on the internet. There are many to choose from. She needs to decide whether she prefers the voice of a man or woman, and to take notice of other features that are advertised. On the CD's, she will be able to listen to the voice of an individual directing her how to carry out the relaxation exercise, following the "tense-then-relax" programme designed by Edmundson. Alternatively, you can make a copy of yourself speaking on a CD, or you can just memorise the exercise as I describe.

A concluding note

I am well aware, from my own experience in my early twenties, that you may wonder whether you and your client are wasting time for two to four weeks by learning the art of relaxation. Your client will quite naturally be keen to get to "the meat" of this method of overcoming her anxiety and/or phobia or panic attacks.

I cannot stress enough, however, that you are helping her to lay the groundwork for the systematic desensitisation programme by learning to be able to control the tension in her muscles. She will be able to use this skill daily in the process of recovery, and it is essential that she learns this skill as thoroughly as possible before she moves on to the next stage.

In Chapter Seven I will go on to describe more about the systematic desensitisation programme.

The systematic desensitisation programme

Introduction

This series of exercises is known as a cognitive behavioural programme—in short, it seeks to help you as a therapist to modify your client's current habits in her way of living, and replace them with a new, productive set of habits, that will enable her once again to take control of her life. It necessitates that as her therapist, you help your client to unlearn "bad" habits and relearn a range of new, "good" (healthy, productive) habits, most probably similar to those that she enjoyed when she was able to live her life unimpeded by anxiety, panic, or phobia. While the programme is largely behavioural, you may want to employ some cognitive restructuring and challenging of negative self-statements, in order to help your client achieve her aim of returning to normal living, unimpeded by panic and phobia.

As the therapist, it is your role to stress that your client needs to have become fully conversant with the relaxation exercises before the two of you can embark on the systematic desensitisation programme. It is important for you to appreciate and teach that each stage needs to be carried out in the prescribed order. Maybe it is wise to stress that this is not a race, to see who can finish first. Neither is it a competition or an examination, where your client is going to be marked on how expertly or how quickly she can achieve the targets. I suggest that you familiarise yourself with the sequence of events by reading through this chapter several times concerning the nature of the systematic desensitisation programme (each stage is highlighted in italic script). You will then find that you can "teach" the client the programme in a clearer fashion. I have found it useful to stress to my client that she needs to regard this programme as if it were a temporary "job"— something which is going to involve her full attention for a while; something that well may be a major focus in life for several months. As you will be aware, a new job involves a steep learning curve while you learn new ways. Change, as I am sure you will appreciate as a therapist already, is difficult to actually achieve rather than just consider, and it requires the client to engage fully, and to give time, emotional and physical effort, and retain a sustained level of motivation.

Building a hierarchy

While your client is practising the relaxation exercises, it is wise to encourage her to *give some serious thought to what sort of situations* she at present finds herself avoiding. You now need to explain that rather than continuing with the passive strategy of avoidance, she needs to begin to take on a proactive strategy of "facing the fear, and doing it anyway" (Jeffers, 2014).

Having helped your client to identify what sort of situations and/or places that engender the symptoms of anxiety in her mind and body, you then help her to put these situations into an ascending order of difficulty. Together, you need to *build the hierarchy* from Number One to Number Ten. Guide her to choose for Task One, a situation that she can still manage, or was able to take part in until recently. The thought of carrying it out will undeniably evoke anxious feelings, but not to an overwhelming extent.

For instance, if you have a client suffering from severe agoraphobia, Task One may involve the simple task of walking out of her front door, and down the garden path with the intention of remaining outside for a few minutes. This may sound "simple" to the average person who takes this process for granted every day, but it is a stressful task for the severely agoraphobic individual to contemplate. I am providing this example in order to indicate the level of the difficulty that you are anticipating that the client will be prepared to engage upon at that stage of recovery.

In order to decide what should constitute Task Two, you need to suggest a situation to your client that she will find a little more stressful that Task One; Task Three needs to be chosen so that it is more taxing again. You will have gathered by now that you need to help your client to think up a reasonably wide range of situations that she can carry out in the relevant order according to her particular anxieties and fears. If, for instance, her fear involves the thought of eating in public, you may organise that for Task One she takes along a couple of biscuits to her local park and eat them while sitting on a bench, with strangers around her. You may help such an individual, suffering from a phobia about eating in public, to move gradually through a range of tasks, until she can undertake Task Ten. This may consist of eating out at a pre-arranged time, having booked a table at a restaurant to eat a meal with a friend or partner. When this hypothetical client has accomplished this, she will find that she has surmounted her worst dread, and can once again live her life unimpeded by fear that she is not able to take part in life fully. One of your functions is to encourage your client to practise the tasks, as regularly as finances allow, in order to instil confidence in her new-found capabilities.

There is an old adage which I am sure your mother recited: "practice makes perfect". I prefer to amend this to the following motto applicable for your clients: "practice builds confidence". Do not forget to remind the clients that they do not have to do these new tasks perfectly, without any residual anxiety from the first time that they engage in putting a task from the hierarchy into practice. As the therapist, you can take the individual programme at a speed to suit your client; you need to reassure her that she can expect to feel a little anxious at first. As you will no doubt be aware, it is in fact normal for anyone to feel a little anxious when engaging in a situation to which they have not been accustomed recently. It is your role as well to encourage the client to persevere, and "get back on the horse, having fallen off" when she encounters some setback. It is useful at the review of each task after its completion to talk through strategies that will help your client to surmount her problem areas when completing the task again. This often may involve some cognitive restructuring of her thought patterns.

I help my clients to build a hierarchy by having a pad of paper, and jotting down the possible tasks, and then starting to order them in ascending order of difficulty. This will involve some discussion, so expect to amend the hierarchy a number of times before being satisfied with it. Then give the client a copy of the hierarchy, and, of course, keep one copy for yourself as an aide-memoire. I find that it sometimes helps the client if she *copies it out on to a neat piece of card*, and keeps it somewhere visible—pinned up on the fridge or a bedroom mirror.

Below, I have written a hierarchy that I helped a client to build and then work through. She enlisted my help as a therapist when she had become very anxious about going anywhere public. Trying to find psychodynamic links, I discovered that some months previously, Yvonne had been traumatised by a sexual and physical attack on her person while she was abroad on holiday. It may be helpful, in order to appreciate the structure of the hierarchy below, that Yvonne had been alone at the time of the attack, and in consequence found it easier to go out when with another person.

"Yvonne's" hierarchy

1. Drive into town and park the car in the NCP (National Car Parks) car park with which you are familiar. Sit there for ten minutes before driving home.
2. Drive into town with a friend and go for a five-minute walk along the river-side.
3. Drive into town, and go for a ten-minute walk by yourself.
4. Go into town with a friend, walk to the High Street (the busy part of town), and visit one shop and make a purchase.
5. Go into town alone, and stop at a shop to make a purchase.
6. Go into town and have a coffee and a cake at a café.
7. Go into town (either alone or with a friend—whichever is most convenient or you find easier), and stay for an hour, walking from shop to shop. Make a few little purchases.
8. Make a reservation for lunch at a restaurant, with a friend for company, and enjoy a meal together.
9. Go to a different town (with which you are not so familiar), and walk around the shops for an hour.
10. Go to a nightclub with a friend for the evening.

The next stage: visualisation of the tasks

The next stage of the programme involves helping the client to engage in a process of *visualisation*. This means that you explain to her how to think about the task that she is going to undertake by imagining every detail she can think about, but from a positive stance. Before each visualisation, it is essential that you encourage the client to carry out the relaxation exercise, so that she is calm in mind and body before she starts the visualisation. You then need to arrange with the client that after *practising the visualisation of Task One a number of times*, she will decide (before her next scheduled appointment with you) to complete the task in the outside world. At this point, you will be able to explain why it was so important for your client to have built up the skill of being able to relax at will. It is good to encourage your client to engage in both the preparatory visualisation process, and the actual tasks, a number of times because this will enable her confidence in her abilities to grow.

At this point, I will give you an example of how a client may complete Task One. Assume that the client is suffering from severe agoraphobia. You need to encourage her to carry out the relaxation exercises first before each stage in order that she will be in as relaxed a state of mind as possible. If it is winter, she may then visualise herself putting on a coat, a pair of gloves, and a scarf. The individual will then, dressed ready for a cold winter's day, imagine taking the front door key and opening the front door so that she can walk down the path. She imagines taking each step, enjoying the sense of being out in the open air once again, noticing if the sun is shining or whether there is frost on the grass or branches of the trees. She imagines herself walking to the front gate. The individual imagines herself standing at the gate for a few minutes, then she imagines turning and walking steadily back to the house. Once inside and with the door closed, she imagines taking off her outdoor clothes, and awarding herself a cup of tea and a biscuit or two! She imagines the sense of achievement that will accompany having completed this task.

Throughout the visualisation, you encourage her to *keep her breathing even, and her muscles relaxed*. Having practised the relaxation exercises for several weeks, she will now be well aware of whether her muscles are relaxed or tense. Tell her that if she notices that she starts to become tense, then she should consciously relax her muscles again.

Again, here is the benefit of having carried out the exercises carefully, and having given them time and expended energy on them.

Carrying out the tasks

It is imperative as her therapist to emphasise that before she *carries out the task in her hierarchy, that she practises the relaxation exercises.* To emphasise my point, this will mean that when she begins the task, she will be in as relaxed a state of mind and body as possible. It needs to be explained that when one is anticipating doing something that she associates with stress, she will not feel entirely calm. However, stress like this should not stop her from undertaking the task! If she were to do this, she will tend to put off the task forever. You need to communicate to her that she has to accept that the anxiety associated with the phobia she has developed may well be well-established, and consequently, she is bound to feel a little anxious—and maybe, a little excited—that she is finally doing something positive to rid herself of this anxiety state. However, use some cognitive restructuring techniques to inculcate the idea that she is not only going to "try the task", she is going to "succeed"!

Once relaxed, the client once again visualises the task that together you have set up for one day in the coming week. *She then proceeds, as calmly as possible, to carry out the task.*

You need to remind her in the session previous to this event, that she must remember to maintain the muscle relaxation, and adopt a way of thinking positively by using mantras such as "This is an important step towards my recovery!", "I am going to get over this anxiety and go back to a normal way of living. Imagine how much better my life will be!"

Remind your client in this session before the task completion, to remember too her rate and depth of breathing—it is important that she keeps the correct balance of oxygen to carbon dioxide. It is all too easy when tense to forget the normally automatic function of breathing, and to either hold one's breath or hyperventilate. Either way, she will tend to feel light-headed if she does this. You need to stress that she is aiming to breathe in a normal, relaxed fashion; at a regular pace; not too deeply and not too shallowly.

You need to arrange your sessions with your client in order to help her to *gradually work her way up the hierarchy, meeting with her after the first time she completes the task (if possible) to review how the event affected her*, and to encourage progress, and *celebrate achievement*. Over a period of weeks or months you are gradually going to move up through the hierarchy—each time, practising the relaxation exercises before visualising the task several times, and then move on to complete the task in actuality. As I have said before, you may persuade your client to *practise each task a couple of times* before moving on to a task higher up the hierarchy. By completing each task a number of times, this will serve to increase her confidence.

The review

Once your client is back in the safety of home, it is important that you encourage your client to think through what parts of the task went well, and what parts (if any) she found difficult. Stress that she should really congratulate herself for completing the task. Here it is useful if she has a close friend, colleague, or partner to share in her success. If she has no such support mechanism, maybe she could telephone you or text you to tell you her thoughts and feelings. At the succeeding session, before you move on to plan the next task, *remember to review the task accomplished*. Much can be learnt from this, both by yourself as therapist and by her.

Working through the hierarchy

Gradually, by carrying out the same process regarding each of the tasks in the hierarchy—relaxation, visualisation practice, task, review—*you together will work through the hierarchy until she reaches Task Ten*. You will then be able to celebrate her return to being able to take part in "normal living" again!

Well done! As a therapist, I find this an immensely satisfying way of working. One is privileged to be a part of a person's return to being able to fully participate in the world. As you will see in the following chapter, this may mean that an individual who has not left her home for a frightening period of over a year, is once again able to enjoy life. This is truly amazing!

The next two chapters focus upon two case studies of individuals with whom I have worked, using a systematic desensitisation programme. The first individual suffered from severe agoraphobia and had been house-bound for some time. In the chapter following that, I describe how a client of mine also worked through the programme, and was able to return to normal living after suffering driving phobia after a motor accident.

CHAPTER EIGHT

Case study: using systematic desenitisation to recover from agoraphobia

Introduction

In this chapter I present the first of two extended case studies. This story focuses upon the story of a woman who, in her middle years, started to suffer from severe agoraphobia. This led her to seek me out as a therapist, having learned that I had helped a number of clients suffering from panic and phobia. Together we embarked upon a systematic desensitisation programme. The case study tells of how she set about learning the art of relaxation, and then developed a hierarchy. She proceeded to visualise the tasks, each in their turn, and to carry them out in the external world with my help and encouragement. I will say a little about the psychodynamic history of her life, which perhaps led her to suffer from agoraphobia so badly.

Psychodynamic history

Carole had been brought up by parents in the North East of England. Her parents had worked together in the family business (a retail establishment), and had left her—as elder sister—in charge of her younger sibling. By the age of ten, she had become adept at preparing and cooking the evening meal. She would return from school, let herself and her sister into the house, and first of all clear up the remains of breakfast and put dirty laundry in the washing machine. She would then prepare the evening meal—often a casserole, or chops and vegetables—and start to cook it in time for her parents' return from their shop at seven o'clock. It would also be her responsibility to entertain her younger sister, who was five years younger than her.

While her parents never physically or sexually abused her, this seemed to me to constitute a blatant case of emotional neglect. In consequence, she never experienced what it felt like to experience a "secure base" (Bowlby, 1988): to "know" intuitively what it is to enjoy, for an extended period of time, recourse to a "secure base" provided by parents when anxieties are aroused. She had never known the joys of a carefree childhood because she had been forced to take on adult responsibilities long before an appropriate time in her life.

Although she did not have a conscious awareness of this in her adolescent years, she became determined to leave home as soon as she could practically manage it. She met and married one of her first boyfriends, and could see when we embarked upon the psychodynamic aspect of our work together, that a partial reason for this choice to marry had been because it represented a way out of the tortuous lifestyle at home. She soon became a mother to twins, and stayed at home as a full-time mother for some years. However, sadly, her marriage did not survive, perhaps as a result of both her and her husband's motivations underlying their decision to marry. When the girls were eight years old, she became a single parent and felt fortunate that she took possession of the family home. She managed to take on a part-time job as an apprentice in a local hairdressing salon, and gradually she was chosen to go to college and train to become a fully qualified hairdresser.

Then, while both of the twins had "flown the nest" to read for degrees at university, she had tragically been mugged on her way back from work one evening. She was, by then, working in another hairdressers' in a nearby large town. She became very fearful of the journey home on the dark evenings, and it will not be difficult for you to make the connection between this incident and its fateful repercussion of agoraphobia. Over a period of the next few years, she gradually left the house less and less. She gave up her primary interest as a member of a bowling team because she could no longer countenance the walk home in the evening after a match. Her life effectively became increasingly focused in the home. Soon, her reluctance to leave the home became so severe that she found her job too stressful to continue, and resigned. Her partner, with whom she did not live, nevertheless started to subsidise her living costs. She managed partially because she had no mortgage or rent to pay and she made a small income by carrying out administrative tasks for a local builder.

When she contacted me, she had not been outside the house for over a year. Her friendships had faltered, and she was totally reliant upon her daughters and her second partner for shopping and anything that required attention in the outside world. However, I was very pleased to be given evidence of a strong determination to recover, because she was willing to hire a taxi to bring her to her sessions with me. She had not driven for some years, and no longer owned a car. Her daughters both worked full-time, and she felt that she had no close friends on whom she could rely for help. It took enormous courage to leave the house (her only "safe haven"), and even more courage to hire the weekly taxi service. Fortunately she had known the man who owned the local taxi firm and he was available for a reasonable fee because he was semi-retired.

While suffering a mugging is sufficient to have severe ramifications on anyone, nevertheless, I believe that Carole's attachment history played a significant part in her personal story. First, she had been forced to take on adult responsibilities long before an appropriate age, and additionally she had not only been responsible for herself but for her younger sibling as well. In addition, her parents appeared to be both embroiled in their family business, to the extent where they did not supply the secure base that she needed in order to grow up happily. I believe that as a result of this developmental deficit, Carole lacked the emotional resilience to deal with the incident of mugging when it occurred. As a proponent of attachment theory, I strongly believe that our mental health difficulties are not only a result of intrapsychic conflict (as Freud propounded) but that environmental influence is just as important in the makings of an individual's psychopathology. It is not so much that some of us sail through life and suffer no periods of crisis. However, some individuals, especially those who experienced the joy of a secure base, have the emotional and physical fortitude to deal with crisis, whereas other individuals who do not have a secure attachment schema, lack the emotional resilience to deal with the vicissitudes of life as they befall them. Some individuals take the route that Carole adopted unconsciously, and withdraw from everyday living. Others of us find our way to a therapist's door at such a point in our life, and rely upon him to supply a reparative experience of a temporary provision of a secure base that one can imbibe until ready to face the world again with an increased sense of security. It may even be that one's psychopathology is resolved. I talk a lot about the effect of knowing what it is to have, or not to have, the experience of a satisfactory attachment experience in my book *Attachment Theory: Working Towards Learned Security* (Fear, 2016). If you are interested in the effect of environmental trauma on the individual, you may enjoy reading this book. The case history of Carole is just one example of many that I could quote from my three decades as a therapist who actually specialises in working in long-term psychotherapy with clients who have suffered developmental deficit and consequently, less than adequate attachment schemas.

Putting the systematic desensitisation programme into operation

After an initial consultation in which I listened to the wide-ranging anxiety symptoms that were ruling Carole's life, I began by teaching her the art of relaxation, using the "tense then let go" model (as described in Chapter Six). We met at weekly intervals over the following month, partially so that I could help Carole to maintain her motivation to practise the relaxation exercises, and partially to enable us to carry out a time-limited version of psychodynamic work, in order to lessen the developmental damage that she had suffered. After four weeks' practice of the exercises twice daily, she had achieved the ability to be able to move from feeling tense to full relaxation within a minute. When she had first practised, it had taken her half an hour to move from tension to relaxation.

Together, we then set about building a hierarchy (as described in Chapter Seven) encompassing many of the situations that caused the panic symptoms to arise that ruled her life. We devised the following hierarchy, having taken into account the reality that Carole had not left the house for a year.

Task One: open the front door, and walk down the garden path to the road. Sit on the garden wall for a few minutes, and then return to the house.

Task Two: take your little dog for a walk down the road for a five minutes' walk.

Task Three: walk to the post office in the village (a ten minute walk) and go inside to buy some stamps.

Task Four: to go further away from the "secure base" of home by going for a longer walk—thirty minutes—to a different side of the village.

Task Five: take the bus in the village and go four stops on it to the next village. You are then to walk the mile to your home.

Task Six: travel by bus into the city centre, and then back again home (a half an hour journey each way).

Task Seven: to go into the nearby city by bus, and once there, to go into a café for a drink and a slice of cake. (This repre sented a huge challenge because Carole had suffered from a phobia about eating outside of the home for some years.)

Task Eight: to go out to a social get-together of the bowls club of which you used to be a member, but where you still have friends.

Task Nine: to go out for a full meal at a pre-arranged time with your partner at a restaurant.

Task Ten: the top of the agenda, to go away for a week-end break to a hotel in the Cotswolds.

We then set about applying the hierarchy practically. Using Task One as an example, she visualised the specific details of undertaking the walk down the garden path. It was winter, so this involved planning to put on a coat, gloves, and scarf, and checking she had the front door key. She then visualised walking down the path. I suggested that she concentrate upon observing the weather; how it felt to be outside in the air; the plants in her garden and the neighbour's garden, too. This served as a distraction. Carole carried out this visualisation a number of times, each time undertaking the relaxation exercises first, until she was capable of thinking about the planned event without becoming panicky.

Carole planned the day before to carry out the actual task on the following morning. Once again, first of all, she carefully carried out the relaxation exercises so that mind and body were suffering no symptoms of anxiety. She then visualised the task, as I have outlined above. Then she set about completing the task. She reported being overjoyed to have voluntarily decided to go out again after so many months. However, I do think this first hurdle was helped by the fact that she had a number of times forced herself to come by taxi to my consulting room.

This encouraged her to move on to the visualisation and eventual completion of the second task. Each time she completed a task, she would practise it again a few times and this enabled her confidence to grow. Carole also made notes about what aspects of the task she had found difficult, and what had been easier to achieve than she had anticipated. It is useful at our review session the following week to discuss the matter, and to do some cognitive restructuring exercises and reframing so that she might tackle similar events in a different frame of mind the next time.

Gradually, over a period of four months, Carole worked her way through the hierarchy as I have described. I encouraged her to practise each task a number of times. By the time that she reached Task Ten (the week-end break) her confidence in her ability to take part in situations that most individuals take for granted had grown so much, that she was able to embark upon it without the foreboding that she had experienced when we set up the hierarchy.

Carole found that she was now free to enjoy life once again. Her world had expanded enormously, from being alone during the day in the confines of her home, to be able to think about taking paid employment once again. In fact, Carole discontinued her sessions with me soon after we completed the hierarchy, but she telephoned me a number of times over the next year, and I was delighted to hear that she applied for, and was given the opportunity to start to work again in paid employment in a hairdressing salon in the village.

This systematic desensitisation programme, carefully followed in sequence, had completely cured her of agoraphobic, panic symptoms. In the next chapter, I will present another case study of a woman with whom it was my privilege to work for a time-limited contract. "Amy" was able to achieve a similar freeing journey that enabled her to return to normal living.

CHAPTER NINE

Case study: using systematic desensitisation to recover from driving phobia

Introduction

T his case study tells us about a woman in her thirties, "Amy", with whom I worked on a short-term, employer-paid counselling contract. This is fortunate, because it serves to prove that huge changes can be achieved within just twelve counselling sessions.

Why was this client suffering from a driving phobia?

Amy asked her employees if she could come to see me because she had started to find it difficult to complete her journey to work every day. In the earlier years of her employment, she had driven herself to her place of work, but for the past three years she had been unable to confront the reality of driving herself anywhere, even within the locality of her home town. Recently, this phobia had grown more pronounced and she now found that she could not even countenance being a passenger in anyone's car. Consequently, she was no longer able to travel to work with a colleague, so she had resorted to travelling by bus. This was highly inconvenient because it involved her changing bus routes in the centre of town in order to take a second bus to reach her office. In consequence, it was taking her an hour and a half to complete her journey to work whereas she had been used to allowing just twenty minutes. Fortunately, she had retained the ownership of her own car, and this gave her access to the practice entailed in helping her to recover from her driving phobia.

First of all, I helped her to explore the psychodynamic roots of her driving phobia. In fact, it was very easy to make the links from past events to the development of phobia. In a way, it was a slightly delayed reaction that had led to a development of PTSD. Three years previously, she had been a passenger in her partner's car when it collided with another vehicle on a huge roundabout at the other side of the city where she had always lived. Thankfully, she was not hurt, apart from a minor whiplash injury to her neck. However, another passenger in the car had been taken to hospital by ambulance with some severe injuries. I discovered that the underlying meaning of the accident is that she felt out of control when in a car, and this fear grew until she dreaded that on some other occasion she might suffer a severe injury herself, or even death. Using a short-term psychodynamic psychotherapy model, we explored her life-narrative, and found that she suffered from a history of feeling that events were beyond her control during her childhood years, because of the unpredictability of family life as her mother was alcoholic.

It is often the case that a phobia develops as a response to feeling out of control in some way. For Amy, the fear of loss of control had resulted in her gradually avoiding the prospect of driving because she feared having a motoring accident.

Having helped her to make sense of the underlying reasons for her phobic development, we worked briefly in some of the remaining sessions on the events during her childhood that had led to this fear of being out of control. I employed some cognitive restructuring techniques to help her to feel differently about control, so that she internalised her locus of control rather than perceiving it as being external to her. However, the majority of my work with her focused upon putting into practice a systematic desensitisation programme.

In the first session, as well as uncovering the roots of her phobia, I taught her the relaxation exercises, based on the idea of "tense then let go" (as in Chapter Six). She then assiduously practised these exercises twice a day for a fortnight until our next meeting. I had purposefully given us a break of two weeks so that she could assimilate and practice this part of her recovery. I explained, at this first session, the importance of the relaxation exercises and why the skill, once learned, would make such a difference to her recovery and her life thereafter.

In the second session, we talked about the various stages of the development of her phobia, which had culminated in her being unable to travel even as a passenger in anyone's car. I was relieved to ascertain that she was well motivated to recover, and regain a normal pattern of living. By the time that she arrived at my consulting room, she had grown to fear that if the phobia progressed, she might reach a stage where she was even unable to go out of the house if it involved any type of motorised transport. It is vital for all of us who suffer a phobia to be motivated to recover, and not to want to settle to define oneself as "an ill person". Infrequently, you can find as a therapist that a person receives a "secondary gain" from maintaining a vision of herself as "ill". This programme needs to be looked upon as a "job" for several months of your life, as it takes enormous psychological effort and time, and so the individual needs to be sure that she wishes to recover.

It may be hard to comprehend, but there are a minority of individuals for whom the development of a phobia is a relief because it provides a rationale to their friends and family as a way of trying to explain rationally why they are unable to participate in normal living any more. The phobia is then used as an excuse to enable the individual to become a hermit—to willingly consign themselves to a cloistered life in the safety of home for ever more. Thus, as a therapist, I feel it bodes well when I hear that an individual client is truly motivated to recover.

In the second session, we focused upon the building of the hierarchy. We took some time to build the hierarchy, finding ten different scenarios that she would aim to achieve, each a little harder than the foregoing one. Task Ten (the final task) was to involve her travelling fifty miles away alone, including some motorway driving with which she had always been unfamiliar. One of the motivations to carry out this task focused upon a planned visit to her cousin who lived there, and whom she had not been able to visit for several years.

Task One involved her plan to get into her father's car, and with him in the driving seat, go for a short drive—just about 200 yards down the road where they lived. She practised the relaxation exercises, then proceeded to visualise the task a number of times while in a relaxed state of mind. In the intervening week before the next appointment, she had completed the actual task a couple of times. Her father proved to be a useful ally, giving her lots of affirmation and encouragement.

At the third session, she was in joyous mood. She felt that at last there was a way out of "the prison walls" that she had started to build around her life. In the third session we reviewed her achievement of Task One and discussed what strategies she would employ to accomplish Task Two. The earlier part of our discussion (the review) helped to build her sense of confidence in her own capabilities. Task Two involved Amy travelling into the busy centre of the city, and parking the car, still as a passenger with her father driving his car. She achieved this second task by the time we met again, and had practised it twice.

We then moved on during the next few sessions to Amy taking the courageous step first of all of driving her own car just a few hundred metres down the road. She had expressed that she would find this very anxiety-provoking, but with my encouragement, she proudly returned the following week to tell me that she had achieved—at last—being behind the wheel of her own car for the first time in over three years. She was jubilant. Then, in the following week, she achieved the task set of driving into town in the evening, just so that she could acclimatise herself as a driver to the road network. Task Five followed, by her driving the car several miles to the next village: we purposefully chose that she complete Task Five by driving somewhere that she would not encounter a lot of traffic, but where she was not as familiar with the road.

In Week Six, we reviewed her achievement of Task Five, which had the effect of boosting her confidence a good deal. We also set up and discussed the intended completion of Task Six. This was to involve her driving into the city where she lived, during the day, with the express intention of driving round some roads with a busy traffic flow. The task after this, set up and discussed in Session Seven, was to involve Amy driving into the city and then parking the car in a multi-storey car park, followed by a drive home again after a short shopping expedition.

Each week, we reviewed her progress, noting down and discussing any difficulties and finding some ways (via cognitive interventions) to circumvent these from happening again. We then discussed and enabled her to visualise the task next in her hierarchy, agreeing that she would repeat the visualisation a couple of times more before embarking on the task itself. Some of the sessions did not follow each other directly, week upon week, in order to provide Amy with the opportunity to practise the task on two or three occasions.

In Session Eight, we set up her plans to drive on the motorway—something she had not attempted in years. In Session Nine, we reviewed her progress in carrying out this task successfully, and talked through the next task—Task Nine—which involved driving to work at the other side of town, and undertaking the return journey at the end of the working day. She had felt a sense of reluctance to take on this task when we had composed the hierarchy, because it involved what she perceived as "her failure in the past few years to live normally".

In Session Ten, we celebrated her capacity once again to drive to and from work. We also planned for her achievement of the ultimate task (Task Ten), which entailed driving on the motorway for about fifty miles to visit her cousin. As I have said before, Amy was motivated to achieve this because she had been unable to visit her cousin for several years. She had relied upon him to make the journey to drive to visit her, and she wanted very much to repay the effort and understanding that he had shown her.

In the penultimate session—Session Eleven—we celebrated her recovery and used the session for consolidation of her new skills and level of self-confidence. Amy described herself as "being absolutely over the moon" with the change that this systematic desensitisation programme had wrought upon her life.

In Session Twelve, we talked through the meaning of the original accident in her life, and she was now able to see that there was an alternative way of reacting to such a trauma. None of us can hope to live life without some crises at times—that is a part of normal living—but each of us does have a choice of how we deal with a crisis when such an event occurs. The idea of this represented a new level of insight about how each of us chooses to live life. Of course, we also celebrated her regained sense of freedom!

I was very happy to receive a card from her two years later, in which she expressed her gratitude, and stated that she had not regressed to her old, limited life-style when she had been unable to enjoy the freedom to have control over her own destiny.

CHAPTER TEN

Cognitive interventions

Introduction

I have mainly discussed a behavioural intervention in the past four chapters: namely, how to implement a systematic desensitisation programme so that you succeed in helping your clients to change their anxious feelings. I have explained how your client needs to move from using avoidance as her main strategy, and replace that with exposure to situations that she has grown to fear. I have then described, in detail, two case studies where individuals have used this technique with my help and encouragement to recover from the frequent bouts of anxiety and panic attack that they were both suffering.

I have also discussed the use of psychodynamic techniques to supplement this behavioural strategy. However, I leave you to decide, as a therapist who has her own ideology of what combination of techniques works best in therapeutic interventions, whether you will adopt this strategy as I do in my work.

In this chapter, I am going to introduce various ways that you can use cognitive interventions so that you can help to reduce your client's anxiety symptoms. I am sure you are aware that in the current zeitgeist within the NHS, that CBT is the modality of choice. This may suit your chosen theoretical orientation, but whether you assent to this choice by government or not, I expect that you appreciate that part of the reason that this modality is in vogue lies in the fact that it is cheap in terms of the restricted number of hours spent by the therapist with the client. Despite my personal reservations about the efficacy of cognitive interventions if used alone, I nevertheless believe that the adoption of cognitive techniques are frequently very efficacious when dealing with panic and phobia. In consequence, this chapter concentrates upon the use of some cognitive interventions that can be very useful to employ as adjuncts to the systematic desensitisation programme.

Negative thoughts

There exists a wealth of statistical evidence to prove that individuals who suffer from anxiety and panic symptoms are prone to thinking negatively. Below, I list some of the negative thoughts that are commonly experienced:

- Preoccupation with thoughts about *danger*.
- Preoccupation with the *safety* of a planned event.
- Worries about *health*: "Do I have something fatally wrong with me?"
- Worries by the individual about whether their symptoms imply that they are "going mad"/"*becoming insane*".
- *Obsessive, intrusive thoughts* that return time and again.
- A high degree of *self-criticism*.
- Consistent level of worry about *not being perfect*/doing things perfectly.
- A sense of *impending doom*.
- *Difficulties in concentrating*/tendency for the mind to go "fuzzy" or blank.
- Hypersensitivity to *criticism* by others.
- *Mental confusion* and/or forgetfulness.

These *cognitions* have a tendency to set up a number of negative *feelings* about the self, as listed below:

- shame
- guilt

- worry
- frustration
- depression
- anger
- sadness
- loneliness
- fear
- nervousness
- apathy.

As I am sure you are aware as a therapist, there is a strong positive correlation between the way we think, and the feelings that result. This chapter aims to help you to recognise the negative cognitions that your client may be suffering. It may be that until you highlight these thoughts with your clients that they have been scarcely aware of some of the thoughts that keep racing through their minds. Such thoughts are known as "automatic thoughts" because they frequently tend to go through the individuals' minds repeatedly, yet they have no conscious awareness of them. Above, I have listed some of the thoughts that your clients may be suffering from when they arrive in your consulting room for the first time. I will discuss next in this chapter the underlying reasons that individuals tend to develop such cognitive styles.

Tendency to catastrophise

I am highlighting the tendency that some people have to "catastrophise". By this word, I refer to the tendency, when something negative appears on the horizon, to immediately jump ahead in one's minds and decide that the most dreadful scenario imaginable is going to take place. Aware of this tendency, you may recognise that your clients may have a tendency to believe that they can forecast the future. Of course, the reality is that none of us can do this.

Take, for example, a person suddenly finding that she has grown a new mole on her chest. If she tends to catastrophise, she may immediately come to the conclusion that she has developed the most severe form of skin cancer: a melanoma. Then, rather than taking into account that even should the mole be unfortunately cancerous, the reality is that many individuals undergo surgery and enjoy a full recovery, the individual is in a state of catastrophe and jumps to the conclusion that the new mole certainly heralds her imminent death. Consequently, she rushes to the GP the next day, already suffering greatly increased anxiety. If the GP is not sure about the new mole, and refers her to a dermatologist, again she jumps to the conclusion that the diagnosis will certainly be bleak. By this time, the adrenaline is coursing round her body, and she will tend to begin to suffer some new symptoms (as a result of the adrenaline), and a new fear of the fear cycle begins.

When your client starts to become anxious, it can be as a result of starting to catastrophise. If you start to recognise that this is a pattern of thinking that is familiar in your client's cognitions, you can begin to challenge her automatic thought pattern by testing these thoughts against reality. For example, if she thinks that she cannot go on a plane journey to Spain, because the plane is bound to crash, you can discuss issues such as "How often do planes actually crash?". The answer is: "Rarely. Air travel is statistically one of the safest ways to travel." Airplane crashes do make the headlines, as opposed to motorway accidents, but partially this is so because they occur so rarely. They hit the headlines because they involve a large number of people being affected at one time.

Some individuals who have been subject to abuse earlier in their lives—be that emotional, physical, or sexual abuse—tend to catastrophise. This is as a result of learned behaviour. If they have been subject to abusive behaviour from someone close to them when they were young, they may associate this with a certain amount of unconscious excitation; of "feeling alive". I realise that this sounds cynical, but so often, the abuse that was suffered was also associated with some form of "love". In other words, it may have been the only time that they received attention from that particular person, and, of course, this was very welcome if they were generally starved of care. In other words, while part of them was very frightened and repulsed, another part of them craved the attention that accompanied the abuse. As a consequence, they may have grown used to the excitement that accompanies "crises", and be tending to replicate this in their current life by tending to "think themselves into catastrophes". You may recognise that this description applies to your client.

Black and white thinking

A related pattern of thinking can be seen in the client who suffers "all-or-nothing thinking". The individual takes each set-back in life to mean that the end-point will be totally negative. For example, the individual's PowerPoint presentation does not go well at a board meeting. Rather than feel disappointed, but decide to learn from her mistakes so that she can improve her presentation skills in the future, the client will tend to jump to the immediate conclusion that she is about to be dismissed from the board.

This pattern of thinking is often associated with the tendency to have unrealistic personal expectations. The individual holds the belief that she should be able to perform without ever making any mistakes in life. There is a lack of reality-checking that in fact we are each only human; every one of us has off-days; each one of us cannot perform every task we undertake in a perfect manner. If you find your client using a lot of "should's" and "ought's" in her sessions, then maybe it is pertinent to analyse that she is suffering from unrealistic expectations regarding her own performance. You may well appreciate already that she suffers from unrealistic expectations and standards regarding herself that are not in line with her expectations of others.

If you start to analyse your client's common cognitive patterns, I am sure you appreciate that life is most often a series of grey pictures, where most things are not absolutely dreadful or absolutely marvellous. The reality of our lives mostly lies between these two scenarios—in other words, in shades of grey: a shade which is a combination of black and white. Only very occasionally do we have an absolutely wonderful day, or a day when absolute disaster strikes.

If you catch your client thinking this way, which often goes along with the previous tendency to catastrophise, then you need to help her to recognise the negative aspects of this way of thinking and help her to moderate her cognitive patterns.

Trying to be a perfectionist

Maybe you recognise that your client has always wanted to do things perfectly; maybe she felt that her parents were never quite satisfied, or she tells you that on her school reports the following words were repeatedly written: "could do better". It may well be that she is her own worst critic. It is our sense of conscience that helps us to decide what is "right" and what is "wrong". Some people have an overly sharp superego; this is perhaps as a result of upbringing; perhaps a result of genetic predisposition.

As I said in an earlier chapter: you need to help your client to adopt the following mantra: "Be kind to yourself". Explain that none of us get it right all the time. This is a case where if the client has a very positive transference towards you, and tends to "put you on a pedestal", she may think that your life is perfect, and you always "get it right". I have found that it is then appropriate to make it clear that your life has its ups and downs too. Without self-disclosure, it is still possible to say: "Do you not think that I have my difficulties in life, too?" We are all human beings who, essentially because by our very nature we are human, naturally make mistakes at times. Mistakes are forgivable. What is important is that we learn from them. Even top professionals like Andy Murray, the tennis player, lose a match sometimes. In many of his "dead-pan" interviews, Andy frequently comments on what he has learned from a match that has not gone well for him. We all need to learn to accept defeat sometimes, and not to waste time dwelling on errors, except in order to learn from them.

Dealing with criticism

As you read this chapter, it may occur to you that your client hates criticism—and always take it to heart. None of us like criticism—we all find it hard to accept and would rather not hear it, but those of us who have learned to deal with it, do two things:

1. We learn to *assess* the criticism. What parts are justified and what parts are unfair?
2. We decide to *learn* from positive criticism: "What can I do better in future? How can I learn from it?"

If your theoretical orientation is psychodynamic, you will appreciate that this difficulty in your client to take any criticism is probably in evidence in the transference. Others of you, of different modalities, may call it "working in the here and now".

It may not be a case that others criticise your client; it may instead be her own inner voice criticising. If a friend were to be so critical, she would rightly decide (I hope) to end the friendship. You might recognise that your client has a tendency to allow herself to be bullied. You need to draw attention to this tendency, and to work on it with your client.

Distancing oneself from worry

You may recognise that I am describing your client when I talk of some people being "natural worriers" (tending to move constantly from one anxiety to another). Does your client consistently tend to see the world from a "glass half empty" rather than "glass half full" (a pessimistic rather than optimistic perspective)?

You can help your client greatly by guiding her to question and challenge these pessimistic thought patterns by examining them in some detail. You can ask the following type of questions:

- Is what you are worrying about statistically likely to become true? More often than not, the chances of, say, crashing the car or being sick in public, are not at all likely. On the contrary, you probably can find evidence that the dreaded outcome is statistically unlikely to happen. In any case, should it happen, you will probably find that you can cope with it much better than you have anticipated. And you may be relieved that the actuality is nowhere near as frightening or anxiety-provoking as you have dreaded. Examples of this mode of cognitive process may occur in your review sessions, when your client is telling you what she found difficult about the task she has just completed. Here is an opportunity to use your cognitive restructuring skills.
- Are your ideas about an event or the way you are feeling only half-formed? Do you perhaps need to think more clearly, and fully, about the idea?
- Is it helpful to you to suffer from this worry? Some of us think that if we worry about "it", then "it" will not happen—it will somehow, in some magical way, insulate us from the fear becoming a reality. There is no statistical evidence to substantiate this "magical" way of thinking.

- If you are constantly worrying, can you actually take some steps to change things? If so, take the steps. If not, then stop worrying.

Personally, I have found the following three quotations by eminent individuals very helpful during the past twenty years. Perhaps you might find them useful as to use as mantras with some of your clients:

Yesterday is gone. Tomorrow has yet to come. We only have today. Let us begin. (Mother Theresa)

Do one thing every day that scares you. (Eleanor Roosevelt)

Feel the fear and do it anyway (Susan Jeffers, 2007)

This chapter concerns, in essence, the idea that if you help your client to analyse her thoughts, she will find that she tends to think negatively rather than positively. It has been proven that our cognitions stimulate us to feel a certain way; in other words, the individual will tend to experience the negative emotions of shame, anger, guilt, fearfulness, terror, etc. rather than the positive emotions of relief, happiness, gratitude, peacefulness, love, and compassion.

Cognitive restructuring

Psychologist Albert Ellis developed the idea of *cognitive restructuring* in the mid-1950s, and it is a core component of CBT. I have been talking about the way that you can help your client to identify and then challenge her negative cognitions and "self-talk" earlier in this chapter.

By cognitive restructuring, we can help our clients to identify unhappy, negative feelings, and challenge the automatic thoughts that tend to lie beneath them. Bad moods spoil lives, and reduce the ways in which we carry out our jobs effectively or feel satisfied within our core relationships. Cognitive restructuring helps us to live with a more positive frame of mind.

There are essentially eight stages to help the individual recognise negative thoughts and adopt the ideas of cognitive restructuring. You can teach the following in your sessions:

1. Be *aware* of your mood and calm yourself.
2. Jot down on a piece of paper the *situation* that triggered your *negative thoughts*.

3. Become aware of what *mood/feelings* have been set up as a conse-
    quence.

4. Jot down what were the *automatic thoughts* (also known as *hot
    thoughts*) that went through your head. These often go through
    your head so fast, that when you first start to analyse them, you
    find it difficult to consciously recognise them.

5. Identify *what evidence supports* these automatic thoughts.

6. Identify *what evidence contradicts* these automatic thoughts.

7. Now try your hardest to be *objective*: just how much evidence is
    there to support your automatic thoughts?

8. *Observe your mood*, now that you have investigated the situation
    that set these thoughts off in your mind. It is likely that you
    already feel more positive.

Challenging negative "self-talk"

Our clients are rarely aware of this, but each of us is constantly
analysing and interpreting the situations in which we find ourselves,
or are planning to undertake in the near future.

A lot of your client's thoughts are sensible. For example, when she
knows that she has to sit an examination, she may tend to tell herself
that she needs to take time to revise. Similarly, she may tend to
prepare herself for an upcoming interview by practising answering
the questions, or do some research to discover some information
about the company that she can utilise at interview.

However, some of your client's thoughts may be unhelpful, and
skewed towards a negative way of looking at the situation. She may
think about the job interview: "I'm sure not to be offered the job; I
know that I'll make a fool of myself." Similarly, she may think about
the upcoming exam: "I'm bound to fail! I always do!"

This "inner voice" may well perpetuate in her mind whether it is
positive or negative (self-talk). It is unhelpful for our client if they
constantly skew their thoughts negatively. You can help your clients
to learn to *dispute* the negative self-talk. You can teach them to ask
themselves the following questions:

•   What am I feeling and how has this been influenced by my
    thoughts?

- To *reality-test* the thoughts. Look for objective evidence that supports the negativity, and also for objective evidence that supports a positive outcome.
- Put the positives and negatives *into perspective*. Just how likely is the worst possible outcome to happen?
- Decide on *goals* that will help you to think more positively. "What attitude can I adopt that will mean I think more positively about the upcoming event?"

A final note to consider about your client's way of life

Sleep hygiene

When any of us is depressed and anxious, it is very easy to slip into a pattern of disrupted sleep. It is widely recognised by health professionals that depressed individuals tend to wake very early in the morning, and feel unable to get back off to sleep. Others may find that they can identify the pattern of waking in the middle of the night— classically about 2 a.m.—and that they find it difficult to return to sleep again for at least a couple of hours. Troublesome thoughts may plague a person during the night, and it is recognised that difficulties always seem greater and more insurmountable in the middle of the night, primarily because we are unable during the night to do anything positive to alleviate the situation.

There are a number of positive moves that you can suggest that your client makes to maximise sleep potential, as listed below:

- Advise them to stop drinking caffeinated drinks (tea, coffee, coke) after 2 p.m.
- It is wise to turn off any machine that emits electronic light (blue light) at least an hour before preparing for sleep. This includes the TV, tablets, mobile phone, computer, laptop.
  It has been proved that these devices stop melatonin from being formed, which is a necessary hormone to build up in the endocrine system to enable one to fall asleep.
- Advise your client to take some gentle exercise during the day. They need to aim to exercise, for example, walking for at least half an hour five times a week. However, do not suggest that they exercise vigorously within four hours of trying to sleep.

- Heavy meals should be avoided after 8 p.m.
- The next point is difficult to enforce because of the social acceptability of alcohol consumption: none of us should drink alcohol or smoke during the evening. Alcohol is a stimulant in the short-term, but it is depressive in the long-term. It also tends to make the individual need to wake during the night in order to urinate.
- Suggest that your client makes her bedroom dark—you can suggest that she buys black-out linings for curtains or black-out blinds. This is especially important if a part of their job entails working night shifts, and they need to sleep during the day.
- They might like to try to use a fan to block out background noise, and to make the bedroom cool.
- It is important to have the temperature in the bedroom neither too hot nor too cold. It needs to be slightly lower in the bedroom (two to three degrees lower) than in the living area (eighteen degrees is recommended).
- They might like to try to apply their relaxation exercises just after they get into bed. Slow, calm breathing can also help a lot.
- You can recommend that they establish a bedtime routine. It is good to carry out exactly the same routine (e.g., a warm bath and a milky drink, take off make-up and apply moisturiser) every night, and to take twenty to thirty minutes preparing for bed.
- It is useful in order to set the circadian rhythms that one tries to go out in the fresh air for a walk first thing in the morning.

CHAPTER ELEVEN

Seeking help from counsellors, psychotherapists, and psychologists

Introduction

I am aware that this book may be used as a self-help book by some members of the public who are suffering acute anxiety, panic, or phobia, and see it as a possible way of accessing a different form of help. This chapter has been written primarily with those individuals in mind. They may not yet have consulted a counsellor, psychotherapist, or psychologist, but may be thinking of doing so once they have read the contents of this book. It may be the case that as a result of suffering from a phobia such as agoraphobia, it would seem an insurmountable hurdle to find your way to the office of a mental health professional. Nevertheless, I urge you to try.

However, it may be true that some of you would prefer to enlist the help of someone who has a professional knowledge and experience of helping clients with their personal problems concerning anxiety and phobia, especially now that you have read about the use of a systematic desensitisation programme. This chapter aims to help you find your way to the door of a professional who is used to helping those of us who suffer from overwhelming levels of anxiety.

Seeking help in the talking therapies

This first section covers seeking the help from professional counsellors, psychotherapists, and psychologists.

Many of you may find this terminology confusing. You may be asking: what is the difference between a counsellor, a psychotherapist, and a psychologist? I know from my own experience of practising at first as a counsellor, and latterly as a psychotherapist, that many clients have arrived at my door without being able to differentiate between the various professions.

Counselling

Counsellors are generally trained over a two to three year period, attending college, university, or a private training body on a part-time basis. All counsellors, psychotherapists, and psychologists are bound by their professional bodies to continue to undertake some continuing professional development (CPD) each year after they qualify, in order that they update, enlarge, and renew their skills. They are also bound by strict codes of practice by the professional registering body or bodies to which they belong.

Counselling training consists of a number of different modalities (different theories that underlie one's way of looking at mental health problems): these theories then underpin the way one learns to work with clients. Some counsellors specialise in working in one particular way with their clients; this commonly covers those of us who work in a *psychodynamic* format, a *person-centred* (or *humanistic*) format, or a *cognitive-behavioural* format.

In *psychodynamic counselling*, the counsellor will tend to concentrate upon the relationship between the past and the present and help you to gain an understanding about the way in which events in the past are influencing your thoughts, feelings, and behaviour in your present life. This is a good choice of therapist particularly if you feel that your anxiety problems date from early on in your life, and that problems that you encountered as a child or adolescent are interfering with your life now as an adult. Psychodynamic counsellors are particularly trained to look for the triggers that I have mentioned in earlier chapters. Moreover, this way of looking at the world may simply appeal to you. A psychodynamic counsellor will listen carefully and empathically (trying to put themselves in your shoes) and thus help you to explore the nature of the problems that you faced in early life (there may be some specific incident or it may be a more general feeling about your childhood or adolescence). Once having analysed your past difficulties, he will then be able to help you to move on and change the behaviours and ways of feeling and thinking that are proving to no longer be productive ways of living in your adult life.

The relationship with the counsellor is understood to be of great importance in this modality, because you will tend to interact with the counsellor in the way that you do with others in your current life outside the counselling room. He can then use this information in the "here and now" of the consulting room to help you. This part of the relationship is called the "transference" and "countertransference": it is deemed to be important because it helps the counsellor to get in touch with how you respond to others in your daily life. However, your counsellor will also give due precedence to what they term the "real relationship". This refers to the way that you feel about the counsellor, and he feels about you and the development of trust and intimacy between you.

A *person-centred counsellor or humanistic counsellor* does not tend to focus upon the past, but has the belief that what will really help you now is to provide a warm, empathic relationship where you appreciate that you will be respected, treated reliably, and that "what you see is what you get" (known by the counsellor as "congruence"). This way of working is crucial because it helps you to develop a deep trust in the counsellor. Under these conditions, the humanistic counsellor believes that you (the client) possess the innate capacity to develop your full potential. Like all the counsellors, he will help you to talk about your difficulties, and to find a way of coping better with them. Humanistic counsellors avoid being directive (i.e., telling you what to do).

In contrast, a *cognitive-behavioural counsellor* (CBT) does not concentrate upon the relationship between the two of you, and will tend to focus upon the present, and how your behaviour and thought processes in the here and now need to change if you are to recover in the way you wish. The systematic desensitisation programme in this book belongs to the CBT school of thought. I have spoken in earlier chapters about how some of us wish to find the roots of your difficulties (a psychodynamic approach), while others want to focus purely upon changing their current way of living. Cognitive behavioural counsellors believe that our feelings and behaviour are a result of our thoughts (cognitions).

Lastly, in describing the various counselling methods, it is important to mention that many counsellors belong to what is known as the *integrative or eclectic school of thought*. They have been taught during their training about a whole range of different theories, and have decided to use a "metaphorical toolbox" from which they choose the "tool" (particular theory) that it is in the best interests of the client to use at a particular time, because of the personality of the client and the nature of her current problems. I belong to this *integrative* school of thought, having written a number of chapters in books and academic papers on integrative theories (Fear & Woolfe, 1996, 1999, 2000). I have undertaken a long training (six years) in psychoanalytic theory, but earlier in my career I learned other theoretical approaches, and I think it is best to combine all my knowledge in order to help my clients to the best of my ability.

Thus, as I have described in earlier chapters, I adopt a mainly behavioural approach for those clients who are suffering from panic and phobia, but I also integrate this approach with a psychodynamic one, in order to help the individual to tease out the roots of their difficulties (the triggers). I believe this two-pronged way of dealing with this type of problem to be most efficacious.

Psychotherapy

Psychotherapists also belong to the same differing theoretical modalities as do counsellors. Generally, however, they tend to have undergone more rigorous training that has taken longer to work through. They are also qualified to work with individuals in longer-term therapy than most counsellors, although some psychotherapists do adopt short-term adaptations of their chosen approach. Although they may become integrative once qualified, it is a necessary prerequisite of a psychotherapeutic training to have undertaken a long period of study in one particular theoretical modality. However, they will most likely have learned something about other modalities during their training.

As in counselling, they aim to listen to you carefully and respond empathically, and to apply theoretical knowledge to better understand the reasons that you are troubled at this point in your life. They then help you to find ways of changing that will enable you to live your life more productively and contentedly.

Psychotherapists are normally qualified to Masters degree (second degree) level.

Psychologists

Chartered clinical psychologists have undergone a different type of training programme from counsellors and psychotherapists. Each of them has first of all taken a first degree (BA or BSc) in psychology, or alternatively has worked to convert their first degree in another field to cover aspects of psychology (a conversion course). Then, in order to become chartered clinical psychologists they have undertaken a full-time doctorate course to gain the qualification of PhD. (This is not the same as doctors of medicine who have undergone a clinical medical training.) During their time in education at doctorate level, psychologists spend an allocated amount of time in health care settings in order to learn and practise the skills of helping individuals with mental health problems, rather than spending all their time purely gaining theoretical understanding.

Many clinical psychologists work in the NHS, although some do work in private practice. There are different types of psychologists—clinical, occupational, forensic, for example. You may want to seek the help of a *clinical psychologist*.

Clinical psychologists often work in a CBT format, although they do have an understanding of different theoretical modalities.

Fees that you can expect to pay

Generally, counsellors charge the least of these three groups of professionals. Their fee structure may be on a sliding scale, varying according to your financial circumstances. Some counsellors offer concessions to those in financial difficulty and to students. Expect to pay anything from £30 to £50 for each one hour session, according to level of training, length of experience, and geographical location. Each session lasts from fifty minutes to an hour in length. A first assessment appointment may last longer to enable them to discuss whether you wish to undertake counselling with them for a period of time.

Psychotherapists generally charge a little more because it has taken them longer to train; they have invested more energy, time, and money in their training; they have a higher degree of expertise. Expect to pay anything from £40 to £70 per one hour session. Fees vary according to geographical area and local supply and demand for psychotherapists. Their length of time in practice may lead to variations in fees too.

Clinical psychologists generally charge more than psychotherapists or counsellors, and their fee structure ranges from £80 to £150 per hour.

A few counsellors, psychotherapists, and psychologists work in the NHS, but with scarcity of financial provision at the moment, the access for many of us to free mental health care is somewhat limited. The current government has initiated a programme of IAPT—Improving Access to Psychological Therapy—and thus in some geographical areas there is provision in the NHS. However, you are not likely to be able to choose your therapist or the approach they adopt, and so many individuals prefer to pay privately in order to access the sort of help they believe to be best for their needs.

Recent research by the British Association of Counselling and Psychotherapy (BACP) has shown that 28% of the adult population have consulted a therapist, and approximately 50% of individuals know someone close to them who has worked with a therapist.

How do I set about finding a therapist?

Word of mouth is an excellent way of finding a good therapist. However, because individuals who have been clients in the past are often reluctant to talk about their experiences, advice from friends and relatives is not always forthcoming.

You may be fortunate enough to be a member of a private health scheme either independently, or as part of your employee benefits. Such private health insurance sometimes includes provision to consult a counsellor, psychotherapist, or psychologist for a set number of sessions. Please enquire from your health insurer what facilities they are willing to fund before seeking treatment. They will also tend to have a list of specific professionals whom you can consult.

Alternatively, you may be lucky enough to have an employer-paid counselling scheme; this is referred to as an EAP (Employee Assistance Programme). You can then approach your Human Resources department at work, and ask if you can be referred to a counsellor. Some responsible employers have adopted the rationale that the mental health difficulties of their employees are likely to impinge upon capacity to work efficiently, and are therefore interested in providing such a scheme for your welfare. The employer employs an EAP Agency to find you a counsellor within your geographical locality. It is usually agreed that the employer is only told that a member of their workforce (no name) has accessed the service, and no details of the counselling sessions are disclosed to the employer. Counsellors and psychotherapists abide by strict codes of conduct regarding confidentiality, and a good counsellor will always fully explain the boundaries around confidentiality, and conditions regarding cancellation (known as the counselling contract) at a first meeting.

If you are unable to access such a service, and do not have any recommendations from friends or relatives, then the best way to find a counsellor, psychotherapist, or psychologist is to approach one of their professional bodies. You can also study the individual websites of many therapists, or counselling agencies (such as www.counselling-directory.org.uk) on the internet, and choose a therapist who appeals to you.

Details of the professional bodies are provided below:

British Association of Counselling and Psychotherapy (BACP)
BACP House
15 ST. John's Business Park
Lutterworth
Leicestershire, LE17 4HB
Email: bacp@bacp.co.uk
Call: 01455 883300

BACP provide a register of members by region. Profiles state the theoretical modality of the individual counsellor, training undertaken, fee structure, types of problem with which they have experience/in which they specialise.

Members agree to abide to a strict code of conduct, and to have suitable professional indemnity insurance cover. There is also a BACP complaints procedure.

United Kingdom of Council of Psychotherapy (UKCP)
UKCP
2nd Floor, Edward House
2 Wakley Street
London, EC1V 7LT
Email: info@ukcp.org.uk
Call: 020 7014 9955

UKCP provides a list of members, listed by their modality, training etc.

They have 8500 individual members, and have accredited training bodies throughout the country that provide the rigorous training it requires to become a psychotherapist.

They, too, have a strict code of conduct for their members, a requirement for regular CPD, and an agreed complaints procedure.

The British Psychological Society (BPS)
This organisation provides a directory of chartered psychologists.

The British Psychological Society
St Andrews House
48 Princess Road East
Leicester
LE1 7DR
Email: enquiries@bps.org.uk
Call: 0116 254 9568

CHAPTER TWELVE

Summary

In the current economic climate where government is consistently looking for mechanisms by which they can reduce public spending, it is not surprising that we as British citizens should feel the effects of this reduction by the lessening of resources in the NHS. It is politically and morally correct for us all to give due credence to mental health issues, and to stop the deficit comparison that has for so long been active to undermine mental health in comparison to matters of physical health. I am sure, as practising mental health practitioners, you are in full accord with me. It seems to me, therefore, that there ought to be a moral imperative to increase the funding of mental health services, as they have always (since the inception of the NHS in 1948) been underfunded in comparison to matters of physical well-being. While there is plenty of political rhetoric concerning the need for all of us to talk about mental health, and not to allow it to remain a "hidden topic" that is spoken of in whispering undertones, there is unfortunately not a commensurate increase in funding or availability of help for those who suffer from mental health problems.

It is partly with all this in mind that I made the decision to write this book. While planning to write this book, I also took the conscious decision to talk about the mental health problems that I suffered from severely in my early twenties. I hope that by making references to my own experiences, I am contributing to the received wisdom of the day that mental health should no longer be a subject we avoid mentioning, particularly with regard to our personal experience. As a mental health professional, I think it is incumbent upon individuals such as me to put one's head above the parapet, and to speak out, in the hope that others may follow my example. Also, I hope that in view of my own tribulations in life in this arena, I am able to put forward the information in this book in an empathic manner. I have met many other mental health professionals who do not appreciate just how frightening and dreadful it is to suffer a panic attack if they have not suffered such an attack themselves. Theoretical knowledge has to suffice, but I hope that by describing the symptoms from a sufferer's point of view, it has provided a valuable insight. On the contrary, we have all suffered bouts of anxiety in our lives, so it is easier to understand these feelings. I have no doubt that you try as a therapist to use your skills as an empathic listener, but I am hoping that I have been able to increase your empathic understanding by reading this book.

Primarily, I have set out in this book to put forward a way of instructing you as a therapist with a method of helping your client to overcome the debilitating and limiting life-style that one tends to adopt when one suffers from disabling levels of anxiety. The systematic desensitisation programme that I put forward in Chapters Six to Nine aims to provide a method of facilitating your client's recovery. As I have stressed, it is necessary for recovery to motivate your client to try their best to enter into the programme with an enthusiastic mindset. Again, I have stressed numerous times that it is essential that you (and they) carry out the groundwork for this programme, by practising the relaxation exercises repeatedly in the first few weeks of your work together. It is highly likely that it has taken time for your client to develop these symptoms that they are suffering when they arrive in your consulting room, and thus it cannot be expected that there is a magic wand that can be waved to enable them to achieve recovery overnight. How many times during my career have I been expected to wave a magic wand? I wish I had one! You, together with your client, have to put all your energies for a while into planning how she will overcome the "bad", unproductive habit of avoidance, and instead learn the "good" habit of exposing herself to the stimuli that cause her anxious symptoms to arise.

However, before venturing to describe the systematic desensitisation programme, I felt it was fitting to describe the physical, emotional, and cognitive symptoms that arise when anyone is suffering from anxiety. I have also described in some detail the nature of a typical panic attack, listing the likely ways that one thinks and feels during these dreaded times. I hope that you find it helpful that I have offered some information about the physiological reasons that individuals suffer the symptoms that so many do. This is my motivation in describing for you in Chapters Two and Three, the nature of the fight or flight cycle, and the way that the symptoms perpetually return because of the fear of the fear cycle. Some clients find it helpful to be able to understand the biological reasons that they are suffering as they are at the present time. I hope that it is helpful for me to have spoken of the way in which you can tackle the likelihood that your client has a certain trigger from earlier years—this could be in childhood, adolescence, or in adult life. As a consequence, I guess that it can be useful to use some psychodynamic interventions, so that together with your client, you can find a different way in today's world that she can react to her personal trigger, whatever that may be. Others of you may prefer not to work in this manner, and may want to concentrate upon a cognitive or behavioural way of overcoming your client's anxiety symptoms. The whole of the systematic desensitisation programme is based upon a behavioural rationale; specific cognitive interventions that you can use are detailed in Chapter Ten.

I found it brought me relief to be able to label my mental health issues in my early twenties. I was immensely reassured to find that many others suffer in the same way that I was suffering at the time. In consequence, I have devoted a chapter to describing the different types of phobia, anxiety states, and OCD that are most common in today's society, so that you can be sure of recognising the different phobias and anxiety states that individuals present with in the consulting room. Also, I thought you may find it useful to know a little about the medications available, both from the medical profession and available to your clients over the counter in local pharmacies. However, as I am sure you know—pills will not cure—our client needs to accept that she needs to find a more proactive route to wellness. Nevertheless, I do believe that medication can provide a useful crutch upon which to rely during the darkest days before your client has learned how to master her symptoms.

I sincerely hope that you find this system of dealing with anxiety issues that you encounter in your practice as helpful as I have, both when I was introduced to it years ago in the 1970s as a patient and in the past three decades as a therapist. I remain exceptionally grateful to Anne, the psychologist who aided my recovery. In consequence I have dedicated this book to her.

REFERENCES

Bowlby, J. (1979). *The Making and Breaking of Affectional Bonds*. London: Tavistock.

Bowlby, J. (1988). *A Secure Base*: *Clinical Applications of Attachment Theory*. London: Routledge.

Fear, R. M. (2015). *The Oedipus Complex*: *Solutions or Resolutions?* London: Karnac.

Fear, R. M. (2016). *Attachment Theory*: *Working towards Learned Security*. London: Karnac.

Fear, R., & Woolfe, R. (1996). Searching for integration in counselling practice. *British Journal of Guidance and Counselling, 24*(3): 399–411.

Fear, R., & Woolfe, R. (1999). The personal and professional development of the counsellor: the relationship between personal philosophy and theoretical orientation. *Counselling Psychology Quarterly, 12*(3): 254–262.

Fear, R., & Woolfe, R. (2000). The personal, the professional and the basis of integrative practice. In: S. Palmer & R. Woolfe (Eds.), *Integrative and Eclectic Counselling and Psychotherapy* (pp. 329–340). London: Sage.

Frye, N. (1957). *Anatomy of Criticism*. Princeton, NJ: Princeton University Press.

Frye, N. (1964). *A Natural Perspective*: *The Development of Shakespearean Comedy and Romance*. New York: Columbia University Press.

Holmes, J. (1993). *John Bowlby and Attachment Theory*. London: Routledge.

Jeffers, S. (2007). *Face the Fear and Do it Anyway*. London: Ebury.

O'Sullivan, S. (2015). *It's All in Your Head: Stories from the Frontline of Psychosomatic Illness*. London: Penguin.

Taylor, B. (2015). *The Last Asylum: A Memoir of Madness in our Times*. Chicago: University of Chicago Press.

Weekes, C. (1962). *Self-Help for Your Nerves: Learn to Relax and Enjoy Life Again by Overcoming Stress and Fear*. London: Angus & Robertson.

INDEX